The Logic of Promise
in
Moltmann's Theology

The Logic of Promise
in
Moltmann's Theology

CHRISTOPHER MORSE

FORTRESS PRESS   PHILADELPHIA

Biblical quotations from the Revised Standard Version of the Bible, copyright 1946, 1952, © 1971, 1973 by the Division of Christian Education of the National Council of the Churches of Christ in the U.S.A., are used by permission.

Library of Congress Cataloging in Publication Data

Morse, Christopher, 1935–
 The logic of promise in Moltmann's theology.

 Based on the author's thesis.
  1. Moltmann, Jürgen. 2. Promise (Christian theology)—History of doctrines. I. Title.
 BX4827.M6M67 230 78-54556
 ISBN 0-8006-0523-3

7130G78 Printed in the United States of America 1-523

To my mother,
Lelia Ludwig Morse,
and in memory of my father,
Christopher Stoakes Morse

CONTENTS

PREFACE

This essay examines a proposal in systematic theology. Perhaps a word at the outset regarding what I take to be the proper work of such a discipline is in order.

Like any systematic interpretation, systematic theology attempts to give an intelligible account of the maximum amount of data with the minimum amount of explanatory principles. The primary data to which the theology of the Christian church is committed comprise a tradition of witness in history, through varying cultural contexts, to the God made known in events concerning Jesus of Nazareth. The purpose of such an account is not, as the name "systematic" might seem to suggest, to reduce the life of the Spirit to categories of rational abstraction. Nor is it to camouflage, and thereby domesticate, the subversive character of the church's mission amidst the sufferings of this world by painting that mission in colors merely conforming to some prevalent intellectual (or anti-intellectual!) terrain. What is at stake in this discipline for the church—and I think for the academy as well—is at once a critical and a constructive task: a "testing of the spirits" (1 John 4:1) and an "accounting for the hope" (1 Pet. 3:15).

The proposal examined here is Jürgen Moltmann's bold contention that the biblical tradition of witness exhibits a promissory significance for faith which is the "clue" to the interpretation of every Christian doctrine. This is not the only significance of that tradition, says Professor Moltmann, but it is the "key" one.

Some biblical scholars object at the start to the singling out of any such "clue" or "key" to the interpretative task. They stress instead the variety of perspectives within the canon and caution against making any one of them normative for all the rest. For systematics, or dogmatics, however, the problem is one of demonstrating the inner connections among the doctrines. The particular responsibility is to clarify the internal coherence of the Christian faith and to elucidate the sense in which it makes sense. Christians obviously do not worship the variety of scriptural forms within the canon. They pray to the one God to whom this variety is believed to bear witness. Thus the intent of a systematic inquiry becomes in theology a search for those motifs, generative ideas, or horizons of thought which best permit the unity already implicit within the diversity of the scriptural witness to the one God to come to expression. The question is never whether a systematic theology has been selective in choosing its organizing principles, but how adequate for integrating the broadest possible range of data its particular choices are. Decisions differ. It is a matter of continuing research.

Moltmann's selection of an eschatological horizon as the most comprehensive context of biblical interpretation, and of promise as the most appropriate generative idea for the formulation of doctrine, thus is to be seen as an experiment in working out the implications of one fundamental biblical theme. This proposal has, I confess, intrigued me since I first read about it in *Theology of Hope* over ten years ago. Despite changes in the social and theological climate since that time, and the further development of Moltmann's thought, I remain impressed with the integrative possibilities afforded by understanding theology's classical rationale, *fides quaerens intellectum,* as *promissio quaerens missionem.* But there are, in my judgment, problems in the case which Moltmann presents. These tend to obscure the logical consequences of his claims for promise. The discussion before us attempts to deal with these problems and thereby address a cluster of current issues in theology, particularly on the English-speaking scene.

In earlier forms this material has been submitted as a doctoral dissertation, discussed at pastors' conferences, and presented in the classroom. In each instance I have been instructed by others.

I am especially grateful to the chairman of my dissertation committee, Professor James A. Martin, from whose work I first received the impetus to explore for myself the possibilities of a "new dialogue" between theology and language analysis, and to Professor Paul Lehmann, with whom the happy privilege of being associated for some semesters as first a student and then a Graduate Assistant remains a continuing reminder of the responsibility and integrity of the discipline which is Christian theology.

I am also indebted to those students at Union who listened with uncharacteristic patience to parts of this text in a seminar on the theology of the promise of God and then took me seriously when I said that I would welcome their criticisms.

For their reading of the manuscript and for unsparing assessments both written and in conversation, I thank J. Louis Martyn, James Cone, Gene Outka, and George Hunsinger.

Finally, my appreciation is expressed to John W. Newman, who found time in his doctoral studies for a thoroughly dependable typing of the final copy.

Union Theological Seminary   Christopher Ludwig Morse
New York

CHAPTER I

PROMISE AS
A THEOLOGICAL TOPIC

With the publication of his *Theology of Hope* in 1964 Jürgen Moltmann announced that one of his purposes was "to develop an understanding of 'the revelation of God' that is eschatological insofar as it attempts to uncover the language of promise."[1] My aim in these pages is to assess Moltmann's accomplishment of this task and to rethink the implications of such a project.

The wording of Moltmann's statement of purpose presents us with a concise index of the range of his concerns and at the same time provokes a number of questions which are crucial for the discipline of systematic theology. What, for example, may be said to constitute the development of *an understanding* in a theological context? Must interpretations of faith meet specific requirements in order to qualify in this regard? And what is entailed in the thesis that an understanding of revelation should be *eschatological*? Can eschatology, as an alleged biblical perspective, be defined with conceptual precision; and even if it can, what significance does such a perspective hold for the present day which justifies giving primacy to it in constructive theology? The reference to *the language of promise* I find especially fascinating, both from a scriptural standpoint, and in light of the attention which has been given to promise as a "speech-act" by certain analytical philosophers.[2] What for Moltmann, we must ask, is the language of promise, and how does one proceed, in his words, *to uncover* it? If indeed the task is to develop an eschatological understanding of the revelation of God by uncovering the language of promise, then clearly everything depends upon what such "language" is considered to be and what methods are employed

1

to arrive at its meaning. These questions are far reaching, and like Moltmann's thought itself they cut across biblical, philosophical, and theological boundaries. This discussion of them will focus upon only one of the subjects which Moltmann has addressed, *the revelation of God,* but it is the account given of this one foundational topic in any theology which is decisively formative for all the others.

In undertaking an analysis of Moltmann's claims regarding revelation the guiding intention here is to determine the issues involved in making "the promise of God" the key to a systematic theological perspective. What are the possibilities and limitations of such a position? Why and how does it matter? To pursue this line of inquiry we need not impose criteria for assessment which are alien to Moltmann's thought, but rather ask how adequate his argument is in terms of the standards for theological interpretation which he himself affirms. Moltmann's originality or lack of it is not our theme. He is not the only one, as we shall see, who has written on this subject. What he has written is not presented as a conclusive and comprehensive systematic theology of promise. His work does, however, represent the most developed discussion available on this particular topic in recent theology. As a catalyst for theological debate in the last dozen or so years no one text, I think it accurate to say, has received more comment on an ecumenical and international scale than has *Theology of Hope.* We can be grateful to Moltmann for opening up the question of a promissory theology in a fresh and vital manner. Gratitude in this instance may best be expressed through criticism. It is the desire to come to some decision about the theological significance of "promise" for Christian faith today, rather than any wish to defend or refute Moltmann's thought as such, which motivates this study.

To anticipate, I shall contend that the case which Moltmann offers for understanding revelation as promise lacks conceptual coherence. There is a logical inconsistency between the biblical view of revelation in the mode of promise which Moltmann adopts and the thought forms which he uses to explicate its contemporary theological meaning. Yet the usual criticism of Moltmann in English-speaking circles that his failure lies in an inadequate appeal to experience I also find to be unacceptable. Alternative proposals more in keeping with the exegetical and logical claims that can be made for promise are required.

But before turning to these matters we must look briefly at the matrix of ideas which has given rise to promise as a current theological topic. We must ask what importance this topic has.

ESCHATOLOGY RECONSIDERED

The context of Moltmann's work is to be found in the resurgence of interest in eschatological and apocalyptic themes which came to prominence in German theology in the nineteen sixties.

Among systematic theologians other than Moltmann the most influential contributors to this development have been Wolfhart Pannenberg, Gerhard Sauter, and Johannes Metz.[3] Their initial reflections on eschatology do not comprise a uniform school of thought. Each of them has followed a course somewhat distinctive from the others, and their work continues today in independent directions. They are to be viewed together more because of their common concern in the sixties to interpret the eschatological character of Christian faith, than for any single interpretation itself. Of the various dimensions to this endeavor the one that relates most directly to our subject is the emergence of emphasis upon "promise" as a key to theological insight. Pannenberg, Sauter, and Metz, as well as Moltmann, have each stressed in his own way the critical importance of this concept.

Pannenberg was the first of this group to introduce the idea of the promise of God as a systematic principle. In an essay in 1959, "Redemptive Event and History," the notion of promise and fulfillment is employed in an attempt to redefine the meanings of the terms "revelation" and "history" and to demonstrate their inseparability.[4] The biblical God, it is argued, is disclosed to the chosen people in making and fulfilling promises with reference always to what is happening in and to the world. This action evokes in response a human awareness of the significance of worldly events which is properly to be designated as "history." A people who live by the promise of God and look to events for the confirmation of that promise have a sense of history. "The tension between promise and fulfillment makes history."[5]

Pannenberg's search in this early essay is for a unified view of reality which allows equally for the meaningfulness of talk both of God's revelation as history and of world events as history. He declares his opposition to the older theological assumptions which posit a dichotomy between divine acts and world affairs and in so doing tend to remove God from ordinary history. At this initial stage of his thinking the promise-fulfillment motif of Scripture provides him with the conceptuality for rejecting both a supernaturalism with respect to God and a naturalism with respect to the world and for contending that neither God nor the world, and with it human existence, can be rightly known apart from the one universal history in which each is involved. "History is reality in its totality."[6]

At the time Pannenberg first presented these views he and Moltmann were associated together in teaching at Wuppertal. Subsequently, it has been Moltmann, rather than Pannenberg, who has more steadily pursued the theme of promise. By 1961 Pannenberg, while still insisting upon the eschatological nature of revelation, had rejected the promise-fulfillment interpretation as being more congruent with older doctrines of revelation as Word than with his own attempts to speak of revelation as history.[7] But in his rejection of this interpretation, as well as in his earlier espousal of it, his arguments have served to make promise a topic of theological debate.

One of the most detailed examinations of promise appears in Gerhard Sauter's text, *Zukunft und Verheissung*.[8] As the subtitle indicates, this study explores the problem of the future in present day theological and philosophical discussion. Sauter maintains that for philosophical inquiry the question of the future has to do essentially with the question of time. When, for example, such concepts as possibility, prolepsis, and freedom are considered, they are treated primarily with reference to temporality. "The problem of the future must be amenable to being integrated into the framework of the theme of time."[9] For this reason philosophy has traditionally been preoccupied with ontology, with the attempt to delineate the logos, or structure, of being. For theology, on the other hand, the question of the future is not in the first instance a question of time but of promise. There is a category difference to be noted. The promise of God is the framework in which theological discussion concerning the future properly proceeds. Because Christians are called to give an account of the ground (λόγος) of their hope (1 Pet. 3:15), theology is responsible for delineating this "logos of hope."[10] Much of Sauter's analysis has to do with pointing out the consequences which follow from recognizing the distinction between a logos of being and a logos of hope. If one thinks of promise *as* the logos of hope, he maintains, this position carries with it logical implications for all theological understanding.[11] As Sauter has subsequently expressed the matter, "Whoever takes as his starting point the category of 'promise' must proceed to the working out of a theological logic."[12]

In the case of Johannes Metz attention has centered primarily on the pertinence of eschatology for the church's practice of mission in a secular world.[13] As a Roman Catholic student of Rahner, Metz is not unaware of the logical dilemmas which post-Enlightenment patterns of thought pose for a Christian doctrine of revelation. He too insists that theologians must think of reality in historical terms and that the classical ontologies of Greek philosophy are inadequate for dealing with questions of hope and the future. But for Metz eschatological thinking, properly carried out, is operational rather than speculative. It serves the cause of mission strategy. It is an ethical stance and not an otherworldly vision. This is demonstrated, according to Metz, by the role which promise plays in the biblical portrayals of revelation. In the Old Testament the words of revelation, he writes, "are not primarily words of statement or of information, nor are they mainly words of appeal or of personal self-communication by God, but they are words of promise."[14] By proclaiming that which is to come they call into question that which now is. As such they do not provide private illumination but create Israel as a social and political entity directed by its hope toward the future. Similarly in the New Testament the death and resurrection of Jesus is "essentially a proclamation of promise which initiates the Christian mission."[15] In the memory of Jesus' suffering faith recognizes the promise of the world's future. But this *memoria passionis* is a " 'subversive remembrance' which shocks us out of ever becoming prematurely reconciled to the 'facts' and 'trends' of our technological society."[16] The appropriate theological response to God's promise, therefore, is not abstract contemplation but reflection aimed at institutional criticism and political activity in the present. For this reason Metz characterizes his point of view as "critical eschatology" or "political theology."[17]

This turn to eschatology, insofar as it is represented by Moltmann,

Pannenberg, Sauter, and Metz, has been prompted by four major factors. From the background of a number of influences which have affected their deliberations the following four contributing conditions especially should be noted.

THE INFLUENCE OF BULTMANN AND BARTH

First, there are the problems bequeathed by Bultmann and Barth. The intention both of Bultmann and of Barth to appropriate the eschatological character of the gospel, against what they took to be its nineteenth-century distortions, is a familiar story. We need only recall Bultmann's reference to the impact created by the teaching of Johannes Weiss during his student days.

> When I began to study theology, theologians as well as laymen were excited and frightened by the theories of Johannes Weiss. I remember that Julius Kaftan, my teacher in dogmatics in Berlin said: "If Johannes Weiss is right and the conception of the Kingdom of God is an eschatological one, then it is impossible to make use of this conception in dogmatics." But in the following years the theologians, J. Kaftan among them, became convinced that Weiss was correct . . . Today nobody doubts that Jesus' conception of the Kingdom of God is an eschatological one—at least in European theology and, as far as I can see, also among American New Testament scholars. Indeed, it has become more and more clear that the eschatological expectation and hope is the core of the New Testament preaching throughout.[18]

Weiss's position with regard to the dogmatic significance of the eschatology which comes to expression in the teaching of Jesus can be stated simply in three propositions. First, it must be granted that the eschatological vision of the gospels involves a cosmology. To think of the kingdom of God merely as a spiritual fellowship, an ethical ideal, or a presently available subjective state—a matter, as Harnack was later to describe it, "of God and the soul, the soul and its God"[19]—is indefensible in light of the gospel account of Jesus' message. The eschatological expectation of the New Testament community assumes the imminent end of the present world. Second, this world view as held by the New Testament community is impossible to accept as such today. Third, what was interpreted originally in cosmological terms must now be interpreted in personal or anthropological terms. "The world will further endure, but we, as individuals, will soon leave it."[20] Only in this shift of interpretation from cosmological to anthropological categories can any present day relevance of biblical eschatology be retained.

Bultmann's program of demythologization, of distinguishing the anthropological, i.e., existential, kernel of the eschatological myths from their cosmological husks, is clearly an advanced development in the tradition of Weiss. But is the anthropological solution to the eschatological problem adequate? The newer eschatological theologies are agreed that it is not. They suggest to us that somewhere between points one and three of his position Weiss may have lost the courage of his best insights.

While Bultmann's attention was drawn to the central fact of eschatology in the gospel by the influence of Weiss, a similar recognition came to Barth by way of the writings of the Blumhardts and, more sharply, Franz Overbeck.[21] The posthumous publication of Overbeck's papers occasioned Barth's early essay, "Unsettled Questions for Theology Today" (1920).[22] Overbeck, in Barth's reading, had denied the possibility of a synthesis between original Christianity and contemporary civilization and had argued that "historic Christianity—that is Christianity subjected to time—is an absurdity."[23] The gospel has to do not with events which can be translated into temporal and historical terms, and thereby attain cultural relevance, but to events which are conceived to be the primal and final boundary (*Urgeschichte*) of all time and all history. This judgment, which led Overbeck to a radical skepticism regarding the prospects for any Christian theology, led Barth to rethink the dogmatic consequences of eschatology. From Overbeck, he writes, "we have the question of the practical significance of the 'last things,' . . . the question of presuppositions. A theology which would dare that passage—dare to become eschatology—would not only be a new theology but also a new Christianity."[24] Barth's often quoted statement in the *Epistle to the Romans* makes his position there unequivocal: "If Christianity be not altogether thoroughgoing eschatology, there remains in it no relation whatever with Christ."[25]

But if in their origins the theologies of Bultmann and Barth vigorously asserted the preeminence of eschatology in biblical thinking, they have proved less convincing in spelling out what such a stance means today. The interpretations which both came to provide, in their increasingly divergent ways, have now produced their own "unsettled questions."[26] These serve as a stimulus for much of the current reappraisal.

With respect to a doctrine of revelation the central difficulty remains that of determining the proper relation of eschatological and historical modes of thought. Are these two ways of perceiving reality finally incompatible, as Weiss and Overbeck concluded, or does each in fact require the other? In their determination to avoid the idolatry of deifying a transient world and mistaking cultural phenomena for divine revelation, both Bultmann and Barth chose to speak of God's self-disclosure in the Word as an "eternal event."[27] The term is curious, each word by definition appearing to cancel out the other. If revelation is truly an *event*, then it would seem to follow that it is an occurrence of time and history. But if revelation is *eternal*, then are not time and history necessarily ruled out? Their reply is that the eternal is not atemporal but has its own time. The time and history which belong to revelation are to be distinguished from the time and history which belong to the world. The individual existence of the believer, according to Bultmann, has its own time and history of revelation.[28] The being of God, according to Barth, has its own time and history of revelation.[29] In both cases an interpretation of revelatory event is offered which tends in an unbiblical fashion, despite explicit qualifications to the contrary, to remove God from the world. Such, in essence, is the critique of the newer eschatological theologians to which we shall return.[30] The legacy of Bultmann and Barth, with both its achievements and its problems, thus constitutes one of the major influences informing their work.

DEVELOPMENTS IN BIBLICAL THEOLOGY

The renewed interest of systematic theologians in eschatology is greatly indebted, in the second place, to what one commentator in 1970 described as an "apocalyptic renaissance" in biblical studies during the past ten years.[31] We refer here not only to the debates over the precise definition of "apocalyptic" in the strict sense, and whether as a literary genre it is more akin to "wisdom" or to "prophecy," but to a broad spectrum of discussion in which, to speak quite generally, ideas of expectation and imminence have been viewed as determinative in shaping the biblical witness. In this wide-ranging body of material the term "promise" often appears.

Once again, to a considerable degree, Bultmann's theories provide a point of departure. In his essay, "The Significance of the Old Testament for the Christian Faith," Bultmann asserts that the Old Testament can be proclaimed as God's Word "only in so far as it is actually promise—that is, preparation for the Christian understanding of existence."[32] Here promise is used as an overall designation of God's Word in the Old Testament, but it is explained solely with regard to an interpretation of faith based upon an existentialist reading of the New Testament. Promise is clearly subordinated to the so-called "Christian understanding of existence." A more explicit statement is provided in the essay, "Prophecy and Fulfillment."[33] When the Old Testament faith in covenant and kingdom and chosen people comes into conflict with Israel's empirical existence, Bultmann argues, this faith becomes eschatological. His thesis is that the idea of promise results because of a "miscarriage of history." "There is nothing which can count as a promise to man other than the miscarriage of *his* way, and the recognition that it is impossible to gain direct access to God in his history within the world."[34] Old Testament history is here given comparable treatment to Paul's view of "the law." Only when it is seen as a "history of failure" does it become the promise of justification by grace. Revelation in this form of promise, therefore, is by definition something apart from world history.

Bultmann's position has met strenuous challenges more recently from among both Old Testament and New Testament scholars. On the Old Testament side the work of Walther Zimmerli, Gerhard von Rad, and Rolf Rendtorff is that which is most often cited by the eschatological theologians. Zimmerli criticizes the existentialist interpretation of promise for not taking seriously enough the historical consciousness of Israel.[35] "When we survey the entire Old Testament," he writes, "we find ourselves involved in a great history of movement from promise toward fulfillment."[36] We are not warranted on this basis to construct a rigid pattern of fulfillments but rather to recognize that each fulfillment serves as a still further promise. Zimmerli concludes by suggesting that systematic theology has yet to develop the significance of the Old Testament promise for Christology.[37]

Von Rad also gives detailed treatment to the connection of promise and history in ancient Israel.[38] The Old Testament, he maintains, allows for only one relationship of Yahweh to Israel, and that is the relationship of "a continuing divine activity in history."[39] Israel's testimonies from one generation to the next of Yahweh's mighty deeds in the world comprise the subject matter of the Old Testament writers. The historical character of their thought, as opposed to the Greek search for the logos of nature's first principles, is evidenced in their overriding dedication to "the proper combination of traditions and their theological interpretation."[40] That interpretation of testimonies and traditions, insofar as the Hexateuch is concerned, is dependent upon the concept of a promised land. The interpretative matrix which makes possible Israel's sense of history in recalling and retelling the patriarchal stories is, in von Rad's account, this "massive arch leading from promise to fulfillment which bridges and spans the whole of the Hexateuchal narrative material."[41]

Rolf Rendtorff similarly finds that the Old Testament affirms Yahweh's self-disclosure to Israel only in the context of historical acts. Yet from the exile on, he writes, the "conclusive self-manifestation of Yahweh was looked for as the decisive event of the future. The earlier patriarchal traditions of sacred history for this reason were not abandoned. On the contrary, they constituted the unconditional presuppositions for the conclusive revelation of Yahweh in the future."[42]

On the New Testament side the break with Bultmann's existentialist interpretation of eschatology is most clearly seen in the writings of Ernst Käsemann and Ulrich Wilkens. Both of these New Testament scholars have stimulated the eschatological trend in systematic theology. Käsemann in this connection is no doubt best known for his thesis that the post-Easter community of primitive Christianity was decisively molded by an apocalyptic consciousness.[43] "Apocalyptic was the mother of all Christian theology—since we cannot really class the preaching of Jesus as theology."[44] When pressed for a precise definition of terms, Käsemann replies: "I speak of primitive Christian apocalyptic to denote the expectation of an imminent Parousia. . . . The beginnings both of Church and theology were conditioned by 'imminent expectation.' "[45] It is Käsemann's contention that this eschatological expectation is clearly indicated in the gospel proclamation of deferred rewards and punishments as it appears especially in Matthew. The commandments of the law are holy and not to be relaxed in the present, but "the community can dispense with any earthly carrying-out of the sentence because it awaits the imminent End."[46]

In addition to this "eschatological *jus talionis*" material, as Käsemann refers to it, in Matthew, we have Paul's teaching on "the righteousness of God." Here again the theme of imminence prevails, with a refusal to collapse the future into present enthusiasm. For Paul the Lord can never become a possession of the believer. "His existence for us," writes Käsemann, "is experienced only according to the mode of promise and can only ever be verified by faith which puts its trust in the promise and which is properly described in terms of παρ' ἐλπίδα ἐπ ἐλπίδι (Rom. 4:18)." Nevertheless, it is important to recognize that the modality of promise does not imply the distance or absence of grace. Quite the contrary, Käsemann states, the righteousness which comes from God is for Paul a living reality. In short, "the divine promise posits reality."[47] Moreover, when the reality of the δικαιοσύνη θεοῦ is understood according to promise it refers not only to the present justification of individual existence but to the coming sovereignty of God over the world as well. Once this is granted the Pauline dialectic of present and future eschatology cannot adequately be depicted, as Bultmann assumes, solely within the context of anthropology. The only appropriate context for an eschatological interpretation including both anthropos and cosmos is mission. "Consciously, and under a sense of apocalyptic pressure, Paul conceived his task to be the universalization of the church's mission. Any interpretation which loses sight of this fails to give historicity its due and therefore minimizes the theological problems with which Paul faces us."[48]

Ulrich Wilkens has also differentiated his approach to the question of revelation in the New Testament from that of Bultmann by insisting that the history in which the biblical God is confessed to be disclosed involves a cosmic as well as an existential dimension. Despite the dissimilarities of ideas in the various New Testament writings, there is common concurrence in the belief that God is revealed in the resurrection of the crucified Jesus. This "historical *Novum*" proclaims both the *person* and the *fate* of Jesus. The distinction between person and the fate or destiny of what happens regarding this person enables us, in Wilkens' view, to safeguard both the historical and the eschatological tendencies in the New Testament conceptions of revelation. "The event that has already been inaugurated will catch up the whole cosmos in a universal way. To this extent, the fate of Jesus is understood in connection with the Jewish-apocalyptic thought as the self-revelation of God. Revelation is the one definitive event as the 'sum' of universal history."[49] Eschatological and historical events are not to be thought of as occurring somehow on two separate levels. Jesus, the historical person, is resurrected to a historical fate as vindicated Lord. Only in the glory of this coming universal vindication in history will God's revelation be complete, but not because, to return to Bultmann's words, of a "miscarriage of history." "According to the apocalyptic view, the future of eschatological self-revelation is the conclusion and ratification of all history."[50] Wilkens thus sets before systematic theology the challenge of conceiving how the history of a particular past can meaningfully be said to become an eschatological future of universal proportions. What conceptual means are suitable for making intelligible the dogmatic significance of such a position for today?

THE PHILOSOPHY OF ERNST BLOCH AND THE CHRISTIAN-MARXIST DIALOGUE

The third influence which has shaped the recent eschatological theologies is the impact of Bloch's left-wing Hegelianism and the occasion of the celebrated conversations in the sixties between Christian and Marxist representatives.[51] Moltmann describes Bloch as "a Marxist with a Bible in his hand, . . . a messianic thinker for whom the philosophy of the younger Marx elicited a practical way to the fulfillment of prophetic promises."[52] He writes, "Bloch's own way of translating eschatological hope into philosophy, in order to make a *docta spes* of it, is as singular as it is unprecedented. His anthropology of 'the not-yet-conscious' and his ontology of 'not-yet-being' bring the first practicable categories into the unknown territory of hope and of the world process."[53] The German text of *Theology of Hope* concludes with an appendix which provides an appreciative critique of the leading concepts of Bloch's *Das Princip Hoffnung*.[54] A Festschrift presented to Bloch in 1965 in recognition of his eightieth birthday contains essays by Pannenberg, Metz, and Moltmann.[55] Sauter devotes a substantial section of *Zukunft und Verheissung* to Bloch's "philosophy of the future."[56] No one among contemporary philosophers has had a greater influence upon the eschatological theologians than has Bloch.

Whether or not Moltmann is correct in claiming that Bloch is the *first* philosopher to speak of hope and world process in "practicable categories," it is the case that his principles have suggested to the descendants of Bultmann and Barth alternative ways of thinking about anthropology and ontology from an eschatological standpoint. There are two main reasons for Bloch's appeal. The first is that as a philosopher, even though Marxist and confessedly atheistic, he has been remarkably interested in the apocalyptic aspects of the Judeo-Christian tradition. And this has been so at a time when an apocalyptic renaissance was occurring in biblical studies.[57] An early work champions the life and thought of the radical reformer, Thomas Münzer.[58] The index to *Das Princip Hoffnung* contains a surprising number of references to the Bible and to figures in church history. The God of Exodus and the Messianic Jesus are recurrent themes in his writings.[59] It is the millenarian heritage of faith and ethics, more often than not suppressed within official Christianity, which in its varied manifestations attracts Bloch's attention. The medieval Joachim di Fiore is a special favorite with his doctrine of the Age of the Father, the Age of the Son, and the coming Age of the Spirit in temporal succession. He is credited with transferring the kingdom from an otherworldly "beyond" into history. "Joachim's utopia," writes Bloch, "like that of the prophets, appears exclusively in the mode of a historic future, as the status of such a future. Joachim's elect are the poor, and they are to enter paradise in the flesh, not only as spirits."[60] This quotation indicates the second reason for Bloch's appeal. He is committed to developing the significance of his eschatological perspective in world-historical terms without recourse to talk of a suprahistorical plane of spiritual reality running parallel to this one. Split-level thinking is rejected in his humanistic materialism. Interpretation is confined to a horizontal scale. Transcendence is conceived with regard to the future before us rather than to an eternity above us or within us. "The forward-look has replaced the upward-look."[61] And this brings with it the necessity for revolutionary mission in overcoming the oppression of the *status quo* and in working toward practical utopias where the needs of the flesh as well as the spirit are fulfilled.

Anthropology forms the basis of Bloch's program. *Das Princip Hoffnung* opens with a lengthy analysis of human subjectivity which stands in sharp contrast to the more generally accepted descriptions of both Heidegger and Freud. Heidegger's existentialist phenomenology of the human being, appropriated in so much of contemporary theology, is judged to be misconceived. His "sociological ignorance" is blamed for the "metaphysical dilettantism" of his attempts to locate the essence of human selfhood in anxiety and the threat of nothingness.[62] On the other hand, Freud's psychoanalytic theories mistakenly seek human identity in the recognition of the power of the past. The unconscious is depicted as the "no-longer-conscious" *(Nicht-Mehr-Bewussten)*, and identity results from a "dawning of that which lies behind" *(Dämmerung nach rückwärts)*.[63] Contrary to both, Bloch holds that the primal anthropological datum is our "anticipatory consciousness" of the future, a hungering hope, which is evidenced throughout human existence in such ordinary activities as day dreams, projections, youthful play, and productivity.[64] The unconscious is seen as the "not-yet-conscious" *(Noch-Nicht-Bewussten)*, and identity results from a "dawning of that which lies ahead" *(Dämmerung nach vorwärts)*. This form of consciousness is attuned to the new. It has a "utopian function" which Bloch examines with respect to such related topics as interest, ideology, archetypes, ideals, and allegory-symbols.[65]

The ontological counterpart of the "not-yet-conscious" is the "not-yet-being" *(Noch-Nicht-Seins)* of the dialectical world process. "The *Noch-Nicht* characterizes the *tendency* in the material process."[66] It is not solely an anthropological category. In Bloch's vision the dynamic of world reality itself displays openness and possibility. "Concrete Utopia stands on the horizon of every reality; real possibility surrounds to the last the opening dialectical tendencies-latencies."[67] The hope of which Bloch speaks is not an easy confidence about the outcome of the future. No mechanism predetermines the outcome of the dialectical process. The *Noch-Nicht* may lead to all or nothing. The end is not guaranteed, but the possibility is given, and the future which is anticipated exercises creative force within the present. Thus in Bloch's ontology the ordinary notion of causality is reversed. "The real genesis is not at the beginning but at the end."[68] The hope theologians, while remaining critical of Bloch at various points, are indebted to him for some of their most important concepts. Terms such as "not-yet," "possibility," "the Novum," "world openness," "tendencies and latencies," and "the power of the future" are adopted and adapted in the effort to express the contemporary dogmatic significance of scriptural eschatology.

Along with the stimulus provided by Bloch's philosophy must be listed the climate of Christian-Marxist dialogue in which the new eschatological theologies arose.[69] Up until the abrupt Soviet repression of the Dubcek government in Czechoslovakia the sixties was a time of increasing contact and exchange among Catholics, Protestants, and Marxist humanists in Europe. New solidarities developed. "Revolution" became a theological theme. The central problem which emerged to form a common basis for discussion was that of the future. How is the future to be conceived? What is its relation to the present? What is the distinction, if any, between *futurum* and *adventus*?[70] A striking fact, as Moltmann has observed, which came to be recognized as the conversations proceeded was that whereas the Marxists were thinking of a *future without God,* the Christians were thinking of a *God without a future.*[71] Both sides began to reexamine their basic presuppositions and standard formulations in the light of this realization with the urgency of the conviction that they were dealing with a problem which had become especially critical in the present age.

A CULTURAL CONCERN WITH THE FUTURE

The fourth factor, therefore, which went into the making of the eschatological theologies was a prevailing assumption, never seriously questioned at the beginning, that twentieth century culture is distinguished by an orientation toward the future. This belief represents a reading of the mood of the times. A future directedness is considered to be the hallmark of the contemporary *Zeitgeist.* "The modern world," Moltmann writes, "is modern precisely because men are fascinated by a future which so far nowhere has taken place and hence will be new." This is "the unique characteristic of modern times."[72]

The idea of the future is held to be a link between biblical thought and current sensibilities which is equally relevant to both. Metz, for example, finds in the secularity of our culture a disposition to control the future which runs headlong into the future's resistance to be controlled, and he even goes so far as to suggest that "the uncontrollability of the future . . . makes the mystery of its providential origin apparent."[73] Pannenberg, for his part, has revived the question of a natural knowledge of God with his description of God as "the power of the future."[74] In his essay, "Speaking about God in the Face of Atheist Criticism," he acknowledges that "an *existent* being acting with omnipotence and omniscience would make freedom impossible."[75] Existence as a category, he concludes, cannot apply to the God who is the origin of human freedom.[76] Christian theology is offered in the concept of the future, however, an understandable means of affirming that God is a present reality, although not a presently existing entity. "For what belongs to the future is not yet existent, and yet it already determines present experience, at least the present experience of beings who—like man—are orientated towards the future and always experience their present and past in the light of a future which they hope for or which they fear. Thus the future is real, although it does not yet exist."[77] Moltmann, as well, has advocated thinking of the future as a "new paradigm of transcendence."[78] The general conviction underlying these proposals for theological reformulation is that the many-sided concern with facing the future is the contemporary mode of consciousness to which the Christian faith speaks most directly.

These, then, in overview are the four factors which have been most immediately influential in shaping the recent turn to eschatology in German theology.

PROMISE IN CHRISTIAN TRADITION

In the broader context of Christian history there is, to be sure, nothing unusual about a theological concentration upon eschatological themes or, even more specifically, upon the subject of God's promise. The current reconsideration is precisely that, a re-consideration of some of the most perennial issues in the tradition. From the standpoint of hermeneutics especially, to limit ourselves to only one illustration from the tradition, the importance of these matters can be seen from the beginning. In the early church a usual way of relating the Old Testament to the New was by means of typological interpretation. Typology views the Old Covenant as a "type" or "shadow" of the New Covenant. The relation is portrayed as one in which earthly or temporal shadows prefigure heavenly or spiritual realities. The thought-form is akin to that of the Letter to the Hebrews where the priests of the Mosaic law are depicted as "a type and shadow of the heavenly sanctuary" (Heb. 8:5), and the law itself is described as "a shadow of the good things to come instead of the true form of these realities" (Heb. 10:1). But the writer of Hebrews also explains that the New Covenant which Christ mediates is superior to the Old "since it is enacted on better promises" (Heb. 8:6). This raises the hermeneutical question as to whether the relation of the old promises to the new can be understood in the same way as the relation of shadows to reality. Two works in historical theology may be cited at this point to demonstrate the persistence of this question and the importance of the consequences which emerge from it in the tradition. Their very titles serve to focus the issue.

Jean Danielou in *From Shadows to Reality: Studies in the Biblical Typology of the Fathers* examines the patristic exegesis of the Hexateuch in the second to the fourth centuries.[79] Danielou's account shows that the eschatological significance attributed to Moses and the exodus in the Old Testament is generally given a sacramental and even mystical interpretation by the Fathers. The exodus is viewed as a shadow which prefigures the present spiritual reality of the church's sacramental grace. Descriptions of the exodus as a presently available mystical experience depend upon the use of allegory and exhibit the influence of Philo's allegorization of the life of Moses. But while the sacramental and mystical—some would say Platonizing—interpretations of the Old Testament eschatological motifs are the prevailing ones in this period, we also find, as Danielou observes, in Irenaeus and Origen particularly, that the Old Testament eschatological interest in the history of creation and its future is carried over into Christian theology.[80] A tension becomes apparent within typological thinking between the sacramental and mystical understanding of spiritual reality and its form of prefiguration and the more future directed and world oriented understanding.[81] The greater the stress upon history in the interpretation of the eschatological passages the less adequate do the shadow/reality patterns of typology prove to be in expressing the Scripture's meaning.

In a second study, *From Shadow to Promise: Old Testament Interpretation from Augustine to the Young Luther,* James Preus investigates the history of promise as a hermeneutical problem in the tradition leading up to what he describes as Luther's "theology of promise'' in the *First Psalms Course* (1513-1515).[82] There are three sets of distinctions which can be discerned in the material which Preus presents. In highlighting these we are able to see how broad the ramifications of our topic are. The first has to do with Augustine's references to promise; the second, with the medieval principle of scriptural interpretation called ''anagogy''; and the third, with Luther's understanding of *testimonia*.

In the writings of Augustine the word ''promise'' is used in two distinguishable ways. It may refer either to that which is pledged or to the pledge itself—we might say, to the *promised* or to the *promise*. In some passages the word stands for the *grace* already present to us in Christ while in other passages it stands for the *message* which announces the coming of the grace of Christ. Speaking typologically, promise in the first sense is always the reality of Christ's gift, a New Testament reality, and never a mere figure or shadow of it. Promise in the second sense, on the other hand, may be recognized in the Old Testament as well as the New and is primarily, though not, Preus contends, exclusively, figure and shadow.

It is not difficult to locate examples of both usages. The tendency to equate promise solely with that reality which is promised, namely the presence of grace in Jesus Christ, is evidenced in Augustine's discussion in his tract *On Christian Doctrine*, of the *Book of Rules* of Tyconius the Donatist.[83] The fourth century Tyconius, in what is perhaps the first concerted attempt in the western church to devise principles of interpretation for the Bible as a whole, lists seven keys to the meaning of Scripture, the third of which is *De promissis et lege*.[84] Of this third key Augustine writes, ''The third rule is 'Of Promises and the Law,' which may be spoken of in another way, 'Concerning the Spirit and the Letter,' as we have called it when we composed a book on the subject. It may also be called 'Of Grace and Commandment.' ''[85] The category of promise, as we can see, is here transposed into the categories of ''spirit'' and ''grace'' and contrasted with the categories of ''letter'' and of ''commandment.'' ''Out of this promise, that is, out of *the kindness of God (ex Dei beneficio)*, the law is fulfilled, which without the said promise only makes men transgressors.''[86] Left to itself this spirit/letter interpretation tends to become a New Testament/Old Testament characterization. Promise in this first sense is an internal matter, the covenant of grace written by the Holy Spirit upon the heart. It is a correlate of love.

The second tendency does not restrict the meaning of promise to the reality of the fulfillment of the new covenant in Christ. Rather, promise refers to a message in the Old Testament as well as the New which comes by hearing. It is, in this respect, something more external. "It is evident that the grace of God was promised to the New Testament even by the prophet, and that this grace was definitely announced to take this shape—God's laws were to be written in men's hearts."[87] In this second way of referring to promise as a message or announcement of that which is to come Augustine discusses the Old Testament promises. These are of two sorts, the ones which have to do only with things which are "earthly and temporal" *(promissa terrena et temporalia)* and hence can now have only a figurative or allegorical significance for the present day Christian, and the promise which points to Christ. In contrasting this promise of Christ as an Old Testament announcement with the earthly promises of *temporalia* Augustine writes, "Nevertheless, whereas as in the said Testament earthly and temporal promises are, as I have said, recited, and these are goods of this corruptible flesh (although they prefigure those heavenly and everlasting blessings which belong to the New Testament), what is now promised is a good for the heart itself . . . since it is said, 'I will put my law in their inward parts, and in their hearts will I write them.' "[88] The promise of Christ in the Old Testament, while still a message and an announcement of that which is to come, is, unlike the Old Testament's "earthly promises," related to the Christ of the New Testament in a history of connection for which allegorical and typological schemes of exegesis cannot adequately account. The role of "shadow" or prefigurement in this instance is different. One cannot say with regard to the reality of Christ as promised to Israel that the Old Testament is merely the "letter which kills" while the New Testament is the "spirit which gives life." The hermeneutical situation becomes more complex. Promise in this second sense, that of prefigurement, is less a correlate of love and more a correlate of hope.

The tension which exists within Augustine's application of typology, on the one hand, to interpret promise as an internal presence of grace and love and, on the other hand, as an external message of hope for that which is coming continues into the Middle Ages and reappears in the twofold manner in which the rule of anagogy comes to be employed. This so-called "fourth sense" of Scripture, which since the fifth century on generally is accepted along with the literal, allegorical, and tropological (or moral) senses as a principle of interpretation, is designed to account for those things still outstanding which the Scripture leads us to expect. The anagogical sense, therefore, has to do with promise and with hope. As a familiar dictum of the late Middle Ages put it, "The letter lets you know what happened, and allegory what you must believe; the moral sense what you must do, and anagogy what you may hope for."[89] What occurs is that anagogy comes to be explicated in some instances mystically and in others eschatologically. Where it is given a mystical interpretation, it tends to become identified with or closely related to allegory, and promise is usually discussed with regard to the virtue of love for God. Where it is given an eschatological interpretation, the typological and allegorical schemes of interpretation tend to break down, and promise is usually discussed with regard to the virtue of hope. The distinction is not absolute if one is willing to allow, as does Preus, that the mystical *visio dei* is itself a medieval form of "realized eschatology."[90] Nevertheless, major differences follow in the formation of Christian doctrine—whether it be of God's revelation, the grace of Christ, the sacraments and the church, or the life of the Christian in the world—depending upon whether the mystical or eschatological tendency predominates.

To these distinctions, first between promise as internal grace and as announcement conveying grace, and second between promise in the mystical and in the eschatological senses of anagogy, may be added Luther's insight into how the words of promise gain their meaning, and, what is equally important, how they do not. Preus recounts how Luther, who initially relies upon the mystical rather than the eschatological inclination in biblical interpretation, discovers in the concept of "testimony" taken from the Psalms an Old Testament genre for God's communication with his people which leads to an eventual abandonment of the shadow/reality, *figura/figuratum* patterns of typology. When it is God who speaks through his prophets his words are *testimonia* which do not require figurative or allegorical interpretation in order to proclaim a spiritual truth to those who are addressed. The Old Testament testimonies are promises. Luther writes, "God's words are called testimonies because they testify to future goods. They are not the exhibition of present things, but testimonies of future things. And on that account, they make faith to be the substance of future things, not of things which appear. Thus, the grace of God was not yet apparent to the ancients, but it was being prophesied."[91] What Luther's thinking discloses is a new conception of promissory language. The old dichotomy between word and referent, or sign and reality, is not applicable to the promises. A distinction between language which gains its meaning in that way and the language of promise must be acknowledged. Preus explains, "Words, Luther is learning, do not, like [sacramental] signs, need some hidden 'grace' to be 'causal.' Words are intrinsically causal: they cause expectation, fear, doubt, hope, or trust in the one who hears what they say."[92] This understanding of the words by which God is known attains the utmost significance when we realize, as Preus states it, that for Luther "*testimonia*—promise—has thus become the normative meaning of the whole Bible."[93] Or, as Luther himself later puts it in a marginal gloss on Rom. 4:14, "*Fides et promissio sunt relativa.*"[94] The implications of this view of the words of promise and how they function extend beyond the area of hermeneutics and radically alter the standard medieval doctrines of grace and faith. "Grace-as-*intellectus*," Preus writes, "is being thoroughly undermined. . . . Therefore, faith is not the grace of intellectus, but the trust of future things that are promised."[95]

I suggest that what these three sets of distinctions illustrate, namely, the emergence of promise as a problem for shadow/reality patterns of hermeneutics, is directly related to the issues involved in Moltmann's efforts "to develop an understanding of 'the revelation of God' that is eschatological insofar as it attempts to uncover the language of promise." The question is whether in revelation the move "from shadow to reality," in Danielou's words, rests upon the move, as Preus labels it, "from shadow to promise." Can we arrive at an understanding of "spirit" from "letter" without first seeking to uncover the extent to which the "letter" encounters us as promise? Must the *sensus theologicus,* as the Scholastics put it, take into account the *sensus logicalis* of what Luther calls "God's words?" And in attempting to interpret faithfully the relation of God's words of promise to God's reality, how shall theology make use of Käsemann's exegetical insight that, for Paul, "the divine promise posits reality"?[96] The recent eschatological theologies represent a reconsideration of some of the most crucial problems in the tradition.

FROM THE WORDS TO THE WORD

The present day counterpart to the patristic and medieval deliberations over the relation of earthly shadows to heavenly realities is to be seen, *mutatis mutandis,* in contemporary theology's deliberations over the relation of words to God's reality. How are the words which tell of God related to the reality of God? Promise has come to the fore as a theological topic once again because of the appeal which has been made to it by the eschatological theologians in challenging the dominant conceptions of "the Word of God" in twentieth century theology. In Pannenberg the challenge is severe. He rejects outright these theologies of the Word insofar as they offer an "authoritarian theology of revelation." This does not mean that the role of language in revelation, even when revelation is depicted as "history" rather than as "Word," can be overlooked. "But the positive meaning of language and word to be adhered to by theology," Pannenberg writes, "will only be ascertainable through a decided rejection of the authoritarian features of the traditional understanding of the word."[97] Sauter, as we have noted, calls for a delineation of *logos* as promise and contends that this reorientation in thinking carries with it the demand for a new theological logic. And Moltmann, whose view of revelation, unlike Pannenberg's, remains explicitly within the tradition of the "Word of God" theologies, nevertheless criticizes both Barth's and Bultmann's doctrines of revelation precisely on the issue of their presuppositions regarding language. Though they operate from different standpoints these positions, he contends, assume in their account of revelation that "word and reality, word and existence, word and name are congruent, and that truth is experienced in correspondence, conformity, and agreement."[98] Both Barth and Bultmann often characterize God's Word as promise. But are promises to be understood as words of corresponding reference in this sense?

The eschatological theologians are not the only ones who have questioned the patterns of thought which have gone into the making of the major Word of God theologies by directing attention once more to the importance of words and the assumptions held regarding them. In Europe the followers of Bultmann have utilized the language philosophy of the later Heidegger with its emphasis upon the word-character of existence in working out the so-called "new hermeneutic."[99] Gerhard Ebeling, representing this approach, has characterized theology as "the theory of the language of faith."[100] In English-speaking circles the analytical insights of linguistic philosophy in its various forms have led to what has been described as "a new dialogue between philosophy and theology."[101] Other examples could be cited, for much of present day theology exhibits this move from the words to the Word precisely, it should be underscored, in order to speak faithfully and intelligibly of "the Word."[102] The appeal to "the language of promise" attracts interest and merits investigation in this context.

It is not surprising that the linguistic turn in much contemporary theology has intensified the demand for intelligibility which confronts all attempts to buttress theological claims by employing the traditional language of *logos* today. Logos, it is commonly acknowledged, has become so variously conceived that its meaning for Christian theology cannot simply be taken for granted. To some extent, obviously, this has always been the case. Even in the classical and Hellenistic periods of Greek thought, where the conception achieved its currency, it developed a broad spectrum of nuances ranging all the way from mere speech or words to the self-communicating rational principle constituting reality at large—that is, to the Word. This terminological breadth presents a critical problem for Christian doctrines of revelation inasmuch as they have their scriptural basis in the confession that "the Logos became flesh and dwelt among us, full of grace and truth" (John 1:14). This verse Aloys Grillmeier has called "the most influential New Testament text in the history of dogma"; and he warns, "The sources of a theology of this kind have often been sought all too far from the material revealed in the Old and New Testaments—scholars have been misled in particular by the Logos-concept."[103]

By declared intention at least, the eschatological theologians have attempted to arrive at a logos conception more in keeping with biblical perspectives. They have advocated that the role of words associated with revelation in the Old and New Testaments be given a more decisive place in determining dogmatic formulations regarding "the Word." In this connection the following passage from Paul Tillich is instructive:

> The doctrine of revelation has been developed traditionally as a doctrine of the "Word of God." This is possible if Word is interpreted as the *logos* element in the ground of being, which is the interpretation which the classical Logos doctrine gave it. But the Word of God often is understood—half-literally, half-symbolically—as a spoken word, and a "theology of the Word" is presented which is a theology of the spoken word. This intellectualization of revelation runs counter to the sense of the Logos Christology. . . . If Jesus as the Christ is called the Logos, Logos points to a revelatory reality, not to revelatory words. Taken seriously, the doctrine of the Logos prevents the elaboration of a theology of the spoken or written word, which is *the* Protestant pitfall.[104]

In this position, which sets itself in opposition to such doctrines of revelation as are found in Barth and Bultmann, we see, nevertheless, the same problem of relating words and reality—only now from the other side. Instead of human words and God's reality coming into correspondence and conformity in the event of revelation, they are here seen as contraries. The mystical tendency in Tillich's interpretation of the Word as Logos is clearly indicated in a footnote to this passage where, in contrast to the "intellectualization of revelation" in theologies which emphasize written or spoken words, he refers favorably to the model of the "Greek mind" in which "from the beginning to the end, knowledge means 'union with the unchangeable,' with the 'really real.' "[105] From the standpoint of the eschatological theologies such a conception of "the Word" violates the role which words of promise have in biblical accounts of the revelation of God.[106] Can promises be understood symbolically, by Tillich's standards, or perhaps "half-literally, half-symbolically?" Once again, as in the past, the idea of promise creates difficulties for symbol/reality, *figura/figuratum* theories of interpretation and a parting of the hermeneutical ways is reached.

The disagreement of the eschatological theologies with Barth is less apparent than that with Tillich on this point because Barth firmly insists that in the Christian understanding of revelation "Logos" must be defined solely in terms of the Old Testament-New Testament message which culminates in the event of Jesus Christ. "Jesus Christ" cannot be defined according to some otherwise accessible idea of Logos. Logos is not the Word of God apart from the "flesh" of Jesus Christ. "Under the title of a λόγος ἄσαρκος we pay homage to . . . some image of God which we have made for ourselves."[107] To speak of the knowledge of God with respect to the "Word which became flesh" is to speak not of mystical immediacies of union with the divine but of *mediated* knowledge. Thus far, Barth and the eschatological theologies concur.

But how is this mediation of revealed knowledge, what Barth calls this "particular form suitable for us, the creature," to be conceived?[108] In Barth's doctrine the most comprehensive designation for the revelatory form of the "Word which became flesh" is *name*.[109] God has named himself for us in Jesus Christ. In this event of naming in which the knowledge of God is mediated to the creature the human words of proclamation essential to this mediation are, according to Barth, empowered by God to *correspond* to his *eternal* being. "If our knowledge of God is true, our words stand in a correspondence and agreement with the being of God."[110] Between the name of God and the being of God there is a necessary connection, but as one made possible solely by the miracle of grace this necessity is logical only because it is theological.

This Eternal Being is the *Deus praesens*. Therefore, to affirm the agreement of the Name with the Being of God we must say, to quote Barth, "The Word of God is. It is never 'not yet' *(noch nicht)* or 'no longer' *(nicht mehr)*. . . . The same holds also of the Word of God become flesh and therefore time. In every moment of His temporal existence, and also at every point previous or subsequent to His temporal existence, in which He becomes manifest as true God and true man and finds faith and witness, Jesus Christ is the same."[111]

The eschatological theologians, on the other hand, are concerned, as we have seen, to give due regard to the *destiny* of Jesus Christ along with his *person*. Jesus Christ is the same "yesterday, today, and forever" as person, but is his fate also to be understood as eternally the same in like manner? In the judgment of the eschatological theologians revelation discloses not only the person of God as the *Deus praesens* but also the future of God as the *Deus adventus* in the parousia of Jesus Christ. The glorification of God in the coming vindication of Jesus Christ over all things is still outstanding, still future, in a way that Barth's doctrine of God's eternity does not adequately allow. Contrary to Barth, eschatological theologians argue that in a biblical understanding of revelation there must be an acknowledgment that the Word of God not only *is,* but is also *not yet.* Therefore, to follow Moltmann at this point, the form of the mediation by which the knowledge of God comes to us in revelation is more accurately conceived as *promise* than as *name.* To be exact, "the name of God is a name of promise."[112] What would appear to be only a slight alteration in wording leads to some profound differences of interpretation which invite our examination. The logic of naming and the logic of promising are not the same.

We are now ready to turn to the specific claims concerning "promise" put forward by Moltmann. These will be explained and then grouped according to the sorts of issues which they pose. Subsequent chapters will be devoted to analysing the case which Moltmann makes for each of these sets of proposals.

CHAPTER II

MOLTMANN'S CLAIMS CONCERNING PROMISE

It is characteristic of Moltmann's style of argument in *Theology of Hope* that the ideas which he affirms are explained by contrasting them with those which he refutes. His reasoning generally takes the form "not that, but this," and in order to know what he is for we must see what it is that he is against. Accompanying each positive statement we find a polemic directed against some alternative position which is rejected as a prevailing misconception in Christian thinking. Thus the claims which Moltmann makes for promise throughout his writings can best be brought together and set forth in terms of contrasts. These may be summarized under the rubrics of three propositions:

1. The God of the Bible is revealed not in an epiphany of eternal presence but in the form of promise.

2. Revelatory speech concerning God is to be understood not as descriptive-sentences *(Lehrsätze)* but as hope-sentences *(Hoffnungssätze)*.

3. In revelation it is not God's transcendental selfhood *(Ichheit)* which is revealed but God's historical faithfulness *(Selbigkeit)*.

We will look at each of these propositions in turn. Before doing so it is necessary that we be aware of the conditions which Moltmann himself accepts as requisite for the making of claims that are Christian and theological.

THE CONDITIONS FOR THEOLOGICAL CLAIMS

Christian theology, in Moltmann's view, is not a matter of saying whatever one pleases in whatever way one chooses about whatever one conceives the word "God" or its surrogate to mean. Such random and unbounded discourse may be of interest and importance in some contexts, but no claim which purports to be an expression of Christian theology qualifies as such unless it abides by certain "rules of the game."[1] These rules take on an added pertinence in light of the "identity crisis" and the "relevance crisis" with which Christian faith is confronted today.[2]

The *first* requirement is that the biblical message must govern what is said. "Christian theology speaks of God with respect to the concrete, specific, and contingent history, which is told and witnessed to in the biblical writings."[3] "The hermeneutical starting point of Christian theology is therefore the concrete history witnessed to in both the Old and the New Testaments."[4] More exactly, these Scriptures proclaim a culminating event in Jesus Christ which is normative for every Christian interpretation. Both what is announced and what is lived in the name of Christian freedom, Moltmann writes, "must be legitimized through reflection on their ground in the crucified Christ."[5] "Christian theology finds its identity as Christian theology in the cross of Christ."[6] It is the Old Testament/New Testament message, seen as culminating in the story of Jesus' death and resurrection, which is the basis of all Christian theological claims. The particularity of this starting point is one criterion which determines what is Christian.

But "the concrete, specific, and contingent history, which is told and witnessed to in the biblical writings" testifies to one Lord of all. Moltmann agrees with the Barthian dictum that theological reflection moves from the particular to the universal, from the specificity of Israel and of Jesus Christ to an interpretation of reality in general, and never in the reverse direction. "The peculiarity of Christian theology," he explains, "can be defined as follows: *Christian theology speaks of God historically and of history eschatologically.* . . . This unity of particular history and universality, of specific memory and all-embracing expectation, is a peculiarity which we find only in Jewish and Christian thought. As long as this dialectical unity can be retained and meaningfully represented, Christian faith is alive. If the unity breaks down, the Christian faith breaks up into a merely historical memory on the one hand, and new experiences of the absolute and the universal on the other."[7] The first condition of Christian theological assertions is that they arise out of that "thinking between cross and parousia" which is grounded in the particular memory and universal hope of the Bible.[8]

The *second* "rule of the game" is held to be more problematical in some quarters, but it is maintained as stoutly by Moltmann as the first. No claim may be said to be Christian and theological unless a reasoned account of its meaning and truth can be given. Moltmann is no biblicist. He explicitly rejects "revelational positivism," the position that the warrants for theological assertions are exempt from rational accountability, along with theological appeals to supernatural knowledge.[9] "The naked positivity of the Bible and the assertion of revelation in church proclamation are not sufficient. They allow Christian talk of God to appear arbitrary."[10] "Theological knowing . . . does not have a supernatural character, but has the distinctiveness of a remembered knowledge of hope."[11] If the biblical God is Lord of all, then no reality is adequately interpreted until its relation to God is understood. Theological interpretation is distinctive as a science or discipline *(Wissenschaft)* in that it is grounded in scriptural exegesis. As such it is not subservient to any other science or discipline, but it must, if it is to be considered theology, develop its *intellectus fidei* in working association with the other sciences. Privileged and unsupported claims in the arena of rational discussion are not—and this is the point—*theologically* scientific. "For theology also truth and salvation are not accessible in the form of possessions, but only in the form of faith and hope."[12] Such faith and hope do not exist within a vacuum but are instrumental in every process of thought and action. For this reason it must be acknowledged that science *per se* has a theological dimension and that "eschatological faith can come to historical self-consciousness only in conjunction with the sciences."[13]

The necessity of accounting for the meaning and truth of its claims in relation to the knowledge claims of other disciplines gives the theological enterprise its systematic character and exposes it to a risk of vulnerability in the world of modern science which the retreat to traditionalism or inwardness avoids only at the price of becoming incommunicable and socially inconsequential. On this point Moltmann is insistent. "Whoever closes the Bible in order to speak more effectively and contemporaneously no longer has anything to tell his age. Whoever breaks off the conversation with the present in order to read the Bible more effectively finally merely engages in sterile monologues."[14] "The Church needs the Bible for its foundation and public discussion as a check."[15] Or again, this time in specific reference to the resurrection, "We must take care to discover in which horizons and dimensions of thought faith in resurrection can become meaningful and how the directions of its questing can be related to those of our scientific age."[16]

This second rule leads to a bold conclusion: "It is indispensable, if theology is to gain the necessary openness to the world in this regard, that it step forth from the status of orthodox truth-statements *sui generis* and develop a *theologia experimentalis* which subjects itself, together with the modern world, to the *experimentum veritatis*."[17]

To be more exact, a theological claim qualifies as an "understanding," Moltmann holds, only when through its exegetical grounding and rational accountability it addresses life and death questions of theodicy and human identity. This principle, while an elaboration of the need to account for the meaning and truth of theological positions, constitutes in effect a *third* condition for theological claims.

"What is stated by the name 'God' can be understandably demonstrated only when it is expressed in connection with a radical, and therefore unavoidable, questionableness of reality."[18] "It is the task of theology to develop the knowledge of God in a correlation with world-understanding and self-understanding."[19] The questions, How can God be justified in a world of evil, suffering, and death?, and, How can I be justified in such a world?, that is, the theodicy and identity questions, arise from God's revelation. Revelation *as promise* creates these questions and shows them to be a questioning of experienced reality itself. Revelation makes reality questionable. That is why theological statements contribute to an understanding only when they address, at least implicitly, the theodicy and identity questions and show them to be in effect a questioning of the justification for situations as they presently exist.

What should be underscored in this connection is that, according to Moltmann, the conditions for making Christian theological claims derive from the character of revelation itself. Christian theology is a *theologia experimentalis* and a *theologia viatorum* precisely because the God who is revealed through Scripture is not at home with things as they presently are. God's kingdom is coming. The established glory of God's universal vindication is awaited. There cannot be a "theology of the homeland" comprised of orthodox truth-statements which are self-evident and *sui generis*—in short, there cannot be a genuine, as opposed to an illusory, *natural* theology—until the whole land, the whole reality, has become the kingdom. Revelation in the mode of promise directs us toward that homeland and sets us on the way to that new reality. For this reason there must be instead a "theology of the way," of the journey, a theory of mission for pilgrims whose truth-claims along with everyone else's are still subject to experiment and testing. "Christian theology is therefore, even in its very language, according to ancient terminology *theologia viae*, but not as yet *theologia patriae*. That is, it is still the theory of historical action, and not as yet the theory of the *theoria Dei,* the vision of God."[20]

THE PRESENCE OF GOD

This brings us to the first contrast which Moltmann draws, the distinction between the concepts of revelation as an "epiphany of eternal presence" and as "apocalypse of the promised future."[21] The first idea he opposes as essentially a Greek conception alien to biblical ways of thinking. The second he defends as Hebrew, and biblical, and proper. No one thesis is more fundamental to Moltmann's theology than the claim that the God of the Bible is revealed not in an epiphany of eternal presence but in the form of promise. Nor has any element in his thought provoked more criticism. What some of the critics have overlooked is that Moltmann's theory does not deny the *presence* of God in revelation but rather an "eternal presence."[22] Promise is itself a mode of presence, but promissory presence must not be confused with eternal presence. That in essence is Moltmann's point. Nevertheless, the success of his argument depends upon how convincingly this contrast can be elucidated.

Let us observe first what Moltmann is opposing. His position may be summarized as follows. The typically Greek idea of the "epiphany of eternal presence" is attributable first to the fifth century B.C. Eleatic, Parmenides, in whose fragments we find its classic formulation. Parmenides portrays the unity of being as that which remains outside of time and history as the "now, all at once, and altogether whole" νῦν ἔστιν ὁμοῦ πᾶν.[23] Ultimate being in this view is total simultaneity. All that is temporal and historical, all that is past or future, all that has been and is hoped for cannot and does not share in this ultimacy. Such a being, or god, manifests only a permanently established presence unrelated to the contingencies of worldly events. Contemplation of that which is eternally now rather than expectation, anticipation, and hope for that which is future is the appropriate human response for the worship of this god that can do no new thing. As immanent ground and unity of being the "now, all at once, and altogether whole" transcends the world of struggle and suffering and change. This Parmenidean conception is developed by Plato and carried over into all patterns of thought derivative of Platonism. The history of Christian doctrine is not exempt. "In the resistance against what seems to be the deceptiveness of Christian hope Parmenides' concept of God has intruded deeply into Christian theology."[24]

What is the objection to the Parmenidean conception? It beguiles theology, Moltmann believes, into taking either of two turns, both of which run counter to Scripture. On the one hand the epiphany of eternal presence may be interpreted in terms of God's radical immanence in things as they are. The existing world is then viewed as diaphanous to deity. This line of interpretation may assume any number of forms, but it inevitably leads to either the localization of deity, the sacralization of society, or the divinization of the world—results which the Old and New Testaments do not hesitate to condemn as idolatrous. On the other hand the epiphany of eternal presence may be interpreted in terms of God's radical transcendence over the things of this world. "Eternity" is then emphasized as the category most appropriate to a delineation of God's being. When this happens God's time or history, if indeed such expressions are even allowable, are, as we have already observed in Barth and Bultmann, said to be of a different order from human or worldly time and history. This approach leads to that two-level vision of God and the world—what Moltmann calls a "double-track" *(Zweigleisigkeit)*[25] in thinking—that is also, he contends, unwarranted from a biblical standpoint.

The fact of the matter is that the Parmenidean view fails because it does not allow for the revelation of God's imminence. From the eschatological stance of the Bible both *immanence* and *transcendence* are applicable to God only in respect to God's *imminence*. It is this witness to the impending reality of God that is *at* hand (ἐγγύς)[26] but not *in* hand which the Parmenidean view violates.

Thus Moltmann declares that instead of fashioning its doctrines along the lines of a Parmenidean "epiphany of eternal presence" Christian theology should think of revelation as an "apocalypse of the promised future." He writes, "In the final analysis it is always a result of the influence of Greek thinking and questioning when one understands the revelation of God attested in the biblical writings as 'epiphany of eternal presence.' That better characterizes the God of Parmenides than the God of the exodus and the resurrection. The revelation of the risen Christ is not a form of this epiphany of the eternal presence, but rather it makes necessary an understanding of revelation as apocalypse of the promised future of truth."[27]

The Old Testament evidence which is marshaled to explain and support this conclusion rests chiefly upon a comparison of Israel's faith with the "epiphany religions" of her neighbors.[28] Referring to the work of Martin Buber and Victor Maag, Moltmann calls attention to the differences between nomadic and agrarian perceptions of reality. The nomad's religion is expressed not in the veneration of sacred places but in the continual journey. God is perceived in the movement of migration and in the desert wandering. God is not identified with the inexorable recurrence of seedtime and harvest or with any sanctified territory. What is noteworthy, Moltmann suggests, is that even after Israel occupied the land of Canaan the nomadic rather than the more settled agrarian consciousness of reality remained. At least the agrarian instincts which at times infiltrated her life, with their corresponding tendencies toward epiphany religion, were never allowed to usurp and overcome her sense of the wayfaring God of the wilderness. This can be seen in the fact that the stories in which Israel recalled and at the same time reaffirmed her deliverance from bondage by Yahweh in the exodus appear in the Old Testament not merely as records of the past but as anticipations of the future. That is, tradition and memory functioned as promise. Because tradition was understood as promise it resisted all attempts by Israel to appropriate it as a sanction or confirmation of her condition or status at any given time. Rather, the memory of the past pointed in Israel's present to the coming of a Yahweh whose impending

future called into question every present state of affairs. Hence Yahweh's "presence" has to be seen as the presence of One who refuses to
be enthroned, institutionalized, or codified in any present arrange-
ments, but who promises to meet his people as they go forth at his call.

In the Old Testament whenever a word is taken to be the "Word of
the Lord" it has the effect, Moltmann points out, of putting its hearers
on the move. The call to Abraham in Gen. 12:1-3 may be cited as the
paradigm here.[29]

> Go from your country and your kindred and your father's house to the
> land that I will show you. And I will make of you a great nation, and I
> will bless you, and make your name great, so that you will be a blessing. I
> will bless those who bless you, and him who curses you I will curse; and
> by you all the families of the earth will bless themselves.

One's attention in this passage is turned toward the future. The effect
of the message is to institute a journey, and the irony of the message is
that it finds no confirmation in Abraham's present situation. The word
which comes to him contradicts his own situation. It is a word so in-
congruous with their inherent possibilities—both procreative and
otherwise—that Abraham and Sarah fall on their faces laughing![30] The
message to Abraham calls for him to leave "country, kindred, and
father's house." He is directed toward a land which is not presently
available to his experience. He is told of it and promised that he will be
guided to it if he follows, but he begins the journey not knowing where
he will be led.

Moltmann finds a similar pattern of response to the "Word of the
Lord" in the prophetic writings. Here "eschatology" in the strict sense
of an ultimate boundary of expectation embracing all peoples and
nations and encompassing even death itself, first emerges in the Old
Testament. Emphasis is upon the coming "Day of Yahweh" which is
proclaimed as bringing universal judgment and hope. Classical
prophecy, Moltmann argues, is consistent with Israel's belief in
promise, while extending its scope. Its eschatological pronouncements
are not to be explained, as some have suggested, as the result of a loss of
faith in the presence of Yahweh.[31] Once again, that sort of explanation
mistakes Yahweh's presence in the form of promise with the notion of
epiphanic or eternal presence.

Apocalyptic further enlarges the boundary of eschatological expectation to include not only peoples and nations but the entire cosmos as well. Moltmann acknowledges the difficulties which the apocalyptic literature presents for the interpreter.[32] The cosmological motifs which are employed appear to cancel out historical and eschatological ways of thinking. To the contrary, he writes, "What is at stake is not a cosmological interpretation of eschatological history but an eschatological and historical interpretation of the cosmos."[33] In other words, the Old Testament vision sees the presence of God as an opening up, an ἀποκάλυψις, of human beings, and nations, and the whole cosmos to the future of God's truth. As von Rad puts it, "From Abraham to Malachi, Israel was kept constantly in motion because of what God said and did, and . . . she was always in one way or another in an area of tension constituted by promise and fulfillment."[34]

From the standpoint of the New Testament the evidence for a promissory understanding of God's revelatory presence, in Moltmann's opinion, is especially persuasive. Paul is the most quoted source here.[35] Referring to Jesus Christ, the apostle writes, "For all the promises of God find their Yes in him."[36] The question is how the "Yes," or the fulfillment, of the promises in Christ is to be interpreted. Does fulfillment mean the annulment of promise? If that is the case, then God is no longer to be known in the mode of promise, and the "apocalypse of the promised future," even if it is an Old Testament conception, does not characterize the revelation of the God of the resurrection. This view Moltmann rejects. Does fulfillment mean only the prolongation of promise? If this is the case, then the revelation in Jesus is merely another manifestation of what has been true all along. Nothing new has occurred except one more step in a historical development. This option Moltmann also refuses to accept. What is needed is an interpretation that provides for both the continuity and the newness which are to be found in the New Testament message. Moltmann's proposal is that the revelation in Jesus Christ is, in his words, the eschatological "setting-in-force" *(In-kraft-setzung)* of God's promise to Abraham.[37] The continuity between the testaments is to be found in the way in which the resurrection makes the historical Abrahamic promise operative as an eschatological process. The Old Testament promise is fulfilled in Christ, not with the result that the promissory form of revelation is rendered obsolete, but with the result that it is enforced with new power—that is, with the power of "the New." Hence Paul writes to the Galatians, "Now we, brethren, like Isaac, are children of promise."[38]

What is new in the resurrection, Moltmann explains, is that the eschatological process which is thereby set in motion is not merely one process among others in world history but rather *the* historical process to which all of world history is finally subject.[39] This in essence is the gospel message. As such the message itself takes the form of promise, as Luther recognized, and as the lexical connection between ἀγγελία (announcement), εὐαγγέλιον (gospel), and ἐπαγγελία (promise) suggests. It proclaims a future of Jesus Christ which cannot be said to have already taken place.[40] But neither is this future remotely distant and without effect in the present. It is no carrot on a string dangling in the sweet bye and bye. What appears in the so-called "Easter appearances" is not "the presence of the eternal" but the presence of a historical dynamic of word and act which promises to overcome all that stands in contradiction to the way of the crucified Lord. "With the raising of Jesus everything has not yet come to pass," Moltmann explains. "With this resurrection an eschatologically determined process of history has come into motion which aims at the annihilation of death through its mastery by resurrection life and which runs toward that righteousness in which God gains his right in all things and the creature thereby his salvation."[41] Only when the aim has been achieved and all that opposes God's will and way has been vanquished will God be "eternally present" in things as they are. But now God is present in the word and process of promise which actively work to disestablish the *status quo* and make room for the coming of the new.

This, essentially, is what it means to say that in the New Testament, as well as in the Old, the God of the resurrection as well as the God of the exodus—for this God is One—is not made known in an "epiphany of eternal presence" but in an "apocalypse of the promised future." According to Moltmann these are two different forms of God's presence which must always be distinguished. As he sums up the matter, "A promise announces a reality which has not as yet arrived. But in announcing this future, the future becomes word-present. . . . I think that we can differentiate here between a presence of God on the way and a presence of God at the goal of the way of promises."[42]

HOPE-SENTENCES

Moltmann's interpretation of Christian theology as a nonaxiomatic *theologia viae*, and of God's revealed presence "on the way" in the form of promise as a "word-presence" of the future, introduces the problem of accounting for speech about that which is imminent, impending, and future. What is the logical status of talk about the *future* of Jesus Christ? How is the significance of such language to be explained? Moltmann addresses this problem directly: "The way in which Christian theology speaks of Christ cannot be the way of the Greek *logos* or of descriptive-sentences *(Lehrsätze)* drawn from experience, but only the way of hope-sentences *(Hoffnungssätze)* and promises of the future."[43] By developing this contrast between what he here calls "hope-sentences" and "descriptive-sentences" Moltmann attempts to show how promise and process may be understood to be related. In doing so he elaborates a second basic theological claim.

The literal translation of *Lehrsätze*—"dogmatic-sentences," or "doctrinal-sentences"—fails to convey what the comparison with "hope-sentences" is really about.[44] *Lehre*, as Moltmann uses the word in this context, refers to any representation or description of an actual state of affairs which is verifiable in terms of present experience. Thus we read, *"Lehrsätze* find their truth in their controllable correspondence to available, experienced reality. The hope-sentences of promise, however, must stand in contradiction to presently experienced reality. They do not result from experiences but are the condition for the possibility of new experiences. They seek not to illuminate the reality which is, but the reality which is coming. Nor do they seek to represent in the mind the reality which is, but to lead this reality into the change which is promised and hoped for . . . By doing this they make reality historic *(geschichtlich)."*[45] *Lehrsätze* become possible, therefore, only after the fact which they serve to re-present. They follow in the wake of present events as if they were bearing the train after reality. In this sense of illuminating that which *is* they are properly to be called "descriptive-sentences."[46] "Hope-sentences," on the other hand, are not to be thought of as the train bearers of reality but as its torch bearers.[47] Their function is not to illuminate where things have been and are but to direct where they are heading. They display a causal quality which descriptive-sentences do not. The distinction between these two types of sentences (though Moltmann does not emphasize the labels *Lehrsätze* and *Hoffnungssätze* in themselves) is crucial to his theory of revelation. He is talking about two kinds of logical significance, although he refers to this contrast in various ways.

What is at stake is the claim that revelation as promise *initiates* the eschatological process of history to which all events are finally subject; it does not simply bring to light some hitherto unrecognized, but nevertheless previously existing, world process. Revelation, in Moltmann's words, "sets going *(setzt),* propels *(treibt),* and conducts *(anführt)*" the process of history.[48] He writes of an "apostolic process of history which God's revelation in promise calls to life."[49] His effort is to indicate the sense in which the language of promise may be said to "make reality historic." This is clearly not just a matter of substituting Heraclitus for Parmenides.[50] An eternal presence of becoming, no less than an eternal presence of being, is contrary to an understanding of historical change which originates in, and is not merely illuminated by, revelation. But how is this revelatory efficacy to be spelled out without finally succumbing to supernaturalism or to the arbitrary assertions of a revelational positivism?

Again we must look at what Moltmann is opposing. There are, as he lists them, three main ways in which Christian theology has traditionally sought to account for its speech about God—the cosmological, the anthropological, and the ontological (or, as Moltmann prefers, the "onto-theological") approaches to the problem of verification.[51] The *cosmological* viewpoint holds that reference to God is necessary in order to make intelligible the unity of the world, either as nature or as history. The cosmos displays a contingency which requires an ultimate grounding beyond itself, and this ground which establishes the world as a coherent whole is what comes to expression in the appearing of Jesus Christ. The *anthropological* approach turns from pure reason to practical reason, from the cosmos to the conscience, and argues that language about God becomes meaningful and necessary in order for human beings to understand themselves. The gospel is true in that it is true to life, in that it addresses what is authentic in the depths of human existence and makes genuine self-understanding possible. Revelation in Jesus Christ thus unifies the human self. The third, *ontological* or *onto-theological,* way of thinking denies that God-talk has meaning only as a unifier of nature and history or as a unifier of personal existence and maintains that such talk possesses a unity and coherence within itself. Human beings can only know God through God, not through the world nor through the self. God alone, not the world nor the self, attests to God in Jesus Christ, and the creature recognizes God in Jesus Christ, as Barth stresses, only through God the Holy Spirit. The unity of God thus revealed in this third position is a tri-unity and must be interpreted along the lines of a trinitarian model.

Now each of these traditional attempts to explain the conditions under which Christian language about God may be said to be meaningful or true Moltmann rejects for a single reason. Despite their differences they all three presuppose that the meaning and truth under consideration must be a matter of the *congruence* between what is said and some available reality—either the world, the self, or God's own being. But the "truth" of a promise, if one may use such an expression, does not reside in any congruence which the promise has with a present state of affairs. A promise requires a future in order to prove itself. In this it differs from naming or describing. What is required, therefore, is an account of Christian speech which recognizes the promissory form of revelation. Cosmological, anthropological, and ontological modes of thought must become eschatological.

The hope-sentences of promise prove to be true insofar as they find fulfillment in the future. Thus they submit only to "eschatological verification."[52] Their efficacy in the present, however, can at least in part be recognized and described. Theology, as Moltmann pursues it, is by intent a description of revelation, and his entire undertaking, as we noted at the beginning, stands or falls with the premise that "the language of promise" can be "uncovered." There is an obvious distinction to be observed between the language of revelation and the language of theology which is used to interpret that revelation—though Moltmann at times fails to distinguish adequately between the two. In his view, nevertheless, it is clear that an eschatological theory of meaning and truth involves a description of what revelation—which itself is said to be nondescriptive—*does* in the present and how it thereby relates to present experience.

This becomes apparent as we draw together the characterizations which Moltmann offers of hope-sentences. *First,* it is claimed that they anticipate the future which is announced in the biblical memories of the past.[53] While *Lehrsätze* express "aspects" *(Aussehen)* of the past, *Hoffnungssätze* express "prospects" *(Aussichten)* disclosed in the past by the tradition of God's promises.[54] Because they point to that which has not yet taken place they require a future in which to demonstrate their truth. *Second,* the hope-sentences of promise are an essential part of the future to which they point in a way that anticipations such as predictions and forecasts, for instance, are not. The words of a promise, unlike the words of a prediction or a forecast, are never dispensable in regard to the reality that they announce.[55] Yet promises also do not limit the new to the possibilities calculated from the present, as do projections. *Third,* since hope-sentences are integral to the future of which they speak, they cause the future to impinge upon the present in the form of a "word-presence." A new state of affairs is initiated, though not completed, and a commitment is entered into. The immediate situation is thereby altered. *Fourth,* by both anticipating and initiating a new state of affairs hope-sentences produce a conflict with things as they are. The greater the new which is expected, and for which room must be made, the greater the conflict which is experienced. For this reason the truth of hope-sentences cannot be considered to lie in an equivalence *(Entsprechung)* between language and present reality, but in a contradiction *(Widerspruch).* What they demonstrate is not their congruence, but their incongruence with existence, not an *adaequatio rei et intellectus* but an *inadaequatio intellectus et rei.*[56] Hence their positive content can be known only by knowing what they negate. The future of Jesus Christ is proclaimed in hope-sentences as the negation of what now are the most universal negations—sin, suffering, and death.[57] Finally, in the *fifth* place, since hope-sentences neither conform to nor confirm things as they presently exist, they cannot be said to derive from a reflection upon experience. The contradiction and incongruence which they produce, however, are prerequisite for an experience of mission and of history. Hence we read, "The titles of Christ . . . anticipate his future. They are not, therefore, hard and fast titles which are fixed on who he was and is, but are, in a manner of speaking, open, gliding titles which announce as promises what he will be. They are, at the same time, dynamic titles. They are motivated and motivating concepts of mission which seek to direct men to their work in the world and their hope in the future of Christ."[58]

In sum, it is Moltmann's contention that the hope-sentences of promise *anticipate, initiate,* and *present* the future, that in so doing they *contradict* the present, and that thus they do not result from experience but *make experience* of mission and of history possible.

TRANSCENDENTAL SELFHOOD OR HISTORICAL FAITHFULNESS?

The foregoing proposals concerning the presence of God and hope-sentences have dealt with the form of revelation. If we move on from the question of *how* God is revealed and ask *what* of God is revealed, the most generally given modern answer, which Moltmann accepts, is that God reveals God's self. The word "self" is the key term here. In opposition to attempts simply to equate revelation with the Bible, or with certain dogmatic propositions or formulations, theology in the first half of the twentieth century heightened the emphasis upon the idea of "self-revelation." John Baillie spoke for a prevailing consensus of thought in this period when he wrote, "God does not give us information by communication; He gives us himself in communion."[59]

The eschatological theologies, working out of this tradition, have pointed to the problem of understanding what "self" or "selfhood" means with respect to God from an eschatological standpoint. To say that God's selfhood is revealed would appear to be more in keeping with conceptions such as "the epiphany of eternal presence" and "descriptive-sentences" than with "the apocalypse of the promised future" and "hope-sentences." Moltmann underlines this point. " 'God himself' *(Gott selbst),"* he writes, "cannot be understood as reflection on his transcendent I-ness *(Ichheit),* but must be understood as his self-sameness *(Selbigkeit)* in historical fidelity to his promises."[60] The contrast he draws is between *Ichheit* and *Selbigkeit,* between God's transcendental selfhood and his historical faithfulness. What would appear at first glance to be only an insignificant and somewhat contrived alteration in wording turns out to be a shift which, in Moltmann's view, necessitates nothing less than a change in the way modern theology has tended to interpret the being of God. We are therefore confronted with a third cluster of claims summarized by the statement that in revelation it is not God's transcendent selfhood which is revealed but God's self-sameness in historical faithfulness.

Here again we see Moltmann's determination to speak of God solely within the context of history and to root out all conceptions of the divine transcendence which are not based upon a biblical recognition of the divine imminence. Whenever transcendence is portrayed in ahistorical or suprahistorical categories it ceases, in Moltmann's judgment, to be governed by the scriptural witness. An eschatological theology would appear to be especially vulnerable in this regard since by definition it purports to focus upon those "last things" which are believed to lie at the end of history, or, some would say, above and beyond history. This notion of the eschaton as ahistorical transcendence Moltmann attacks as a fundamental error which has infiltrated much of the theology since Kant. "It was just this transcendentalist version of eschatology which prevented the break-through of eschatological dimensions in dogmatics."[61]

Kant is singled out as the one most responsible for removing the *eschata* from the realm of knowledge and for restricting the significance of these last things to the level of ethical imperatives.[62] Eschatology by this process, Moltmann explains, loses its cosmological and historical reference points and becomes appropriated by theology only with reference to its practical importance in the decision-making of the human self—a shift, as we have previously noted, from a total world view to anthropology. In reflection upon the structure of the moral act the transcendence of the human self is revealed. In order to understand the limits and possibilities of human experience, both cognitive and moral, a reflective analysis of the self is required. The categories and imperatives which thus emerge are transcendent conditions which are assumed to be unaffected by history. Origin and end are at once the same. From this perspective the terms "eschatological" and "transcendental" become synonymous.

Although the idea of a "self-revelation" of the Absolute was expounded by Hegel in the nineteenth century, the theological or dogmatic impetus to the *Ichheit* conception Moltmann attributes to Wilhelm Herrmann and his influence upon both Bultmann and Barth. The key statement of Herrmann in this connection Moltmann takes to be this: "We cannot know God otherwise than that he reveals himself to us ourselves by acting upon us."[63] The question, as Moltmann puts it, is whether "the 'self' of self-revelation refers in fact to God or to man."[64] For Herrmann the reference, following Kant, is anthropological. God is revealed to the human self in the exercise of its subjectivity. God is thereby "experienced" in non-objectifiable terms. This anthropological stress is maintained in Bultmann's existentialist interpretation, a position which Moltmann labels "the theology of the transcendental subjectivity of man."[65]

Barth, on the other hand, in adopting Herrmann's emphasis upon the self as the locus of revelation, reversed the reference to designate the divine subject rather than the human subject. Herrmann had sought to ground his dogmatic claims in the inviolability of religious experience. In this manner he attempted to speak of revelation dynamically as God's free action upon us. To say that God is a free subject in all dealings with us, and that God is never an object of our cognition or control requires, Herrmann concluded, an acknowledgement of God as triune. But the Trinity, as Schleiermacher had earlier recognized, cannot be said to be a datum that is present in human experience.[66] Thus Herrmann held that "the way to religion," as he termed it, must submit not only to those spiritual realities which are experienced but to the unfathomable mystery of God's triune subjectivity in freedom which alone makes religious experience possible. "It becomes obligatory," Barth wrote in 1925, "to ask whether dogmatics does not have to begin where Herrmann ends."[67] The idea of the triune God who as Eternal Subject is known only through himself, Barth contends, is to be understood as the condition for faith and not as a reflection upon faith. "A wholly different 'Self' has stepped into the scene with *his* own validity. An a-priori of the so-called religion becomes visible *above* all that has been or can be experienced, above all circles and correlations."[68] This view of the divine "Self" Moltmann labels "the theology of the transcendental subjectivity of God."[69] In the case of both Bultmann's and Barth's appropriation of Herrmann, Moltmann argues, a reflection upon a transcendent and suprahistorical "self," in the one instance human and in the other divine, as the locus of revelation is required. Eschatology in each view is given a transcendental rather than a historical interpretation, and it becomes meaningless to speak of the God revealed in Jesus Christ as having any future other than that which now is.

The *Ichheit* conception, Moltmann further asserts, also fosters an exclusively personalistic understanding of revelation which is as incompatible with the language of promise as is an ahistorical transcendentalism. God, in the biblical tradition, discloses not only the name of his I-ness, or person, but the pledge of his constancy and of his vindication in all things. Thus God is known in the keeping of his word as well as in the issuance of it, and the revelation at the end of the way of promise brings something new which is not present in the beginning. "Omega is more than alpha."[70] The City of God is not a return to the Garden of Eden. "The original creation was created out of the will of God," but ". . . the new creation corresponds to the essence of God and is illuminated and transfigured by God's earthly presence."[71] Hence if theology is to speak of the "self-revelation" of God—and this is a useful expression for affirming the divine initiative as a free subject in the revelatory act—then it must recognize that the so-called "self" of God includes a coming kingdom as well as a personal identity. Personalistic and existentialist categories alone are incapable of articulating this eschatological dimension. Revelation is not reducible to I-Thou encounters. A *something* as well as a *someone* is disclosed in the exodus and the resurrection. "To be sure," Moltmann writes, "the Alpha and the Omega are the same with reference to the person. . . . But they are not the same with reference to the reality of the event. . . . Thus something new must be expected of the future. But it is not expected from someone new or someone else."[72] This leads to a conclusion which Moltmann believes has important dogmatic consequences. " 'God himself' cannot mean only God in person, God in his I-mystery, but must also always mean God as God and Lord, God in his lordship-mystery. Where God himself is revealed his lordship and his power are revealed, and his lordship and power are revealed where his promises of blessing, peace, and righteousness are fulfilled by him himself. To know 'I am Yahweh,' and to know his glory which comes to pass are one and the same."[73]

Now it is Moltmann's position that because revelation takes the form of promise, God in his coming kingdom and glory can be said to be *known* in the midst of history and not simply when his word is completely fulfilled at the end. There are partial fulfillments along the way, and these in turn point on beyond themselves as further promises to a yet future realization. "Between promise and fulfillment stretches the process of the history of the working of the word. . . ."[74] The promise of God does not afford a speculative or abstract knowledge of the future, a kind of clairvoyance regarding coming events. But if it is not, in the words of John Baillie, a "communication of information" in this sense, neither is it an immediacy of personal "communion" which can, so to speak, be vertically conceived. Rather we are to think less of a contemplative, mystical kind of awareness and more of a socially "involved," "practical" knowledge[75]—a horizontal knowing of God which can only be described as down-to-earth, or matter-of-fact (sachlich), in that it arises from daily participation in the struggles of Christ's mission in this world.[76] Therefore it is in ordinary events as they occur in mission that God himself as Selbigkeit, in the constancy of his commitment, is made known.

It should here be reiterated that while Moltmann, like Pannenberg, argues for an understanding of "self-revelation" which rejects the allegedly vertical, or transcendental interpretations of "the Word" in favor of more horizontal, or historical ways of thinking, he does not follow Pannenberg in further distinguishing "revelation as history" from "revelation as word." The move from the Içhheit formulations of Bultmann and Barth to a more eschatological and historical Selbigkeit view of God's self-disclosure requires not less emphasis upon "the working of the word," but more. With reference to these former theologies Moltmann writes, "Therein lies not an overestimation of the Word, but an underestimation of the breadth and freedom in which the transforming Word seeks to lead the whole reality."[77] It is strange indeed to find Barth and Bultmann taken to task for underestimating the significance of the Word!

Finally, it must be asked if the Selbigkeit idea of the divine selfhood accords with a trinitarian confession. The Ichheit interpretation arose, we have seen, in the attempt to safeguard the belief in the sovereign freedom of God to remain the initiating subject in the act of revelation. In relating himself to creation, it is said, God discloses an eternal relatedness which is intrinsic to his own being and not dependent upon creation. God is not in essence different from who he is to us in revelation. That is the crucial point. Trinitarian doctrines have generally sought to hold in tension both God's distinction from the world, conceived either as nature or as history, and God's relation to the world as it is revealed preeminently in Jesus Christ. The relation of grace is said to reveal the distinction. This Herrmann acknowledged at the conclusion of his dogmatics, and the recognition marked a starting point for Barth. But if the divine "essence," as Moltmann puts it, includes something new in the end which was not in the beginning, is such a claim consistent with a trinitarian theology? Moltmann believes that it is and that the Trinity must be understood eschatologically as well as incarnationally.[78]

The difficulty in delineating the Trinity in horizontal and historical terms has traditionally been that such efforts have tended to result in thinking of the three persons in metamorphic sequence—first God as Father, then as Son, and then as Holy Spirit—a periodization which forfeits the divine unity of the distinctions, the ancient heresy of Sabellianism.[79] From the very beginning Barth felt the need to speak in classical terms of an internal or "immanent" Trinity in order to guarantee that the threefold character of God's revealed dispensation or "economy" in relation to the world was not a distortion, but a true manifestation of God's own being.[80] However, when the revelatory act is seen, to use the convenient short-hand, horizontally rather than vertically, and *Selbigkeit* takes the place of *Ichheit*, the older distinctions between the "immanent" and the "economic" Trinity lose their validity. Moltmann elaborates this viewpoint in his writings on "the Crucified God." The cross of Christ *sub Pontio Pilato* is not the name or reflection of a divine *Ichheit* transcendent to history but the very being *(Wesen)* of the divine *Selbigkeit* operative in history. Two propositions, therefore, must be maintained: "1. The Trinity *is* the being of God, and the being of God is the Trinity. 2. The economic Trinity *is* the immanent Trinity, and the immanent Trinity *is* the economic Trinity."[81] "This also means," writes Moltmann, "that God's being is historical and that he exists in history. The 'story of God' then is the story of the history of man."[82]

With this reference to the Trinity the primary points which Moltmann develops with respect to the contrast between *Ichheit* and *Selbigkeit* are before us. Three basic propositions have now been introduced. The task is to sort out the issues posed by each of these and then to examine their significance.

THREE SETS OF ISSUES

Our aim to this point has been to give Moltmann a fair hearing, to assemble and review the essential positions which he espouses in his theory of revelation, and to show something of the dimensions of his thought. Now we must undertake to question these positions and to consider the case which he offers in support of his conclusions.

When we look at these three propositions it becomes apparent that several of the same themes find expression in each of them. When we read, for example, that theology does not consist of "truth-statements" which are *sui generis* or axiomatic we are dealing, certainly in one sense, with a linguistic issue. The same is the case when we encounter references to "word-presence," or to "the words of promise," or to "hope-sentences" and "descriptive-sentences." These obviously involve us in unavoidable questions about language. Above all we are concerned to know what exactly "the promise" is and, as we observed at the beginning, to determine what Moltmann means by "the language of promise." We confront the perennial problem of the relation of the Word to the words and of the *sensus theologicus* to the *sensus logicalis*.

But when Moltmann discusses the language of promise he does so always in connection with reference to the term "history." The reason theology is a *theologia viae* and not a *theologia patriae*, we are told, is that it is bound to a history initiated by revelation which is still in the process of fulfillment. The reason that God's presence is not revealed to us as "eternal presence," or that the "apocalypse of the promised future" cannot be transcribed by means of "descriptive-sentences," is that the promise of God makes reality "historic" and open to a still outstanding future. Thus God is known by his historical faithfulness and not by some ahistorical encounter with a transcendental "I." It is necessary to examine, therefore, precisely what Moltmann means by "history." Bound up with this inquiry is the topic of "experience." How are we to understand the insistence that Christian confessions of hope do not result from "experience" and that theology accordingly cannot be based upon "experience"? What, furthermore, is entailed in the thesis that revelation makes "the experience of history" possible?

Clearly this idea of "the experience of history" is at the center of Moltmann's deliberations concerning promise.

Finally, everything which is said about language, history, and experience contributes to an interpretation both of God's being and of the reality of the world. Ontic delineations are inherent in talk of God's presence "in the form of promise," of the "apocalypse of the promised future," and of God's selfhood (and even tri-unity!) as "historical faithfulness." What are the ontological problems that are encountered in attempting to develop an eschatological understanding of God and of the world? How is the relation of promise to the future to be conceived in relation to the world process and to God? With the rejection of cosmological ontologies, on the one hand, and of existentialist, or anthropological, ontologies, on the other, does eschatological ontology offer a third and more viable option for contemporary theology?

The three sets of issues, therefore, to which attention will be directed in the remaining pages are: first of all, the language of promise; second, the experience of history; and third, the question of an eschatological ontology. The logic of Moltmann's position will be studied in regard to each of these subjects. The discussion will be expanded to include other resources as we proceed, but the focus will remain upon Moltmann's theory of revelation, and his accomplishment will be evaluated in light of his stated aim and of the conditions which he himself has set for the making of Christian theological claims.

CHAPTER III

THE LANGUAGE OF PROMISE

The thesis to be examined in this chapter and the next is, in short, that *the language of promise creates the experience of history, thereby revealing God.* In keeping with Moltmann's own stipulations regarding theological claims—namely, that they be governed by Scripture, that a reasoned account of the conditions for their meaning and truth be provided which does not resort to supernaturalistic explanations, and that they be correlated with both an understanding of the world and of ourselves—we must now attempt to determine more exactly what this thesis asserts and what the dynamics are of this "process," as Moltmann calls it, whereby the language of promise *(die Sprache der Verheissung)* creates the experience of history *(die Erfahrung der Geschichte).* Here in Chapter III our analysis shall center on the question of promissory language, and in Chapter IV, on promissory experience and history. But as we have seen, these topics are interrelated in Moltmann's thought, and each must be considered with reference to the other.

PROMISE AS A LANGUAGE-EVENT

If we ask what the "promise" is, the most rudimentary answer we are given is that it is a "language-event." With this general designation we must begin and from here proceed to a more complete description. "A promise is a 'language-event' *(Sprachereignis),* but of such a kind that it preserves the remembered history and aims at the future reality of historical fulfillment."[1] The expression *Sprachereignis* is not Moltmann's invention. It is most commonly associated today with representatives of the "new hermeneutic" theology, particularly with

Ernst Fuchs. Gerhard Ebeling writes similarly of "word-event" *(Wortgeschehen)*. The two terms are used interchangeably, both deriving from Bultmann's concept of "salvation-event," written sometimes as *Heilsereignis* and sometimes as *Heilsgeschehen*.[2] In adopting this expression Moltmann gives his own interpretation to it and in characteristic fashion distinguishes his view from the "new hermeneutic" position. Responding to Ebeling he writes, " 'Promise' is fundamentally something other than a 'word-event' which brings truth and unanimity between man and the reality that concerns him."[3] Thus to define "promise" as a "language-event" is merely to suggest its formal character in theology. A description of what happens in this event is required to supplement this abstract definition in order to explain the kind of *Sprachereignis* that promise is.

Nevertheless, the bare designation of promise as a "language-event" enables us to see that whatever else may be involved, we are dealing here in the first instance with words and with acts which occur through words. The words are those which comprise the telling and hearing of the biblical message. The acts are what take place when this message is told and heard as God's message. Therefore, for Moltmann the word "promise," in its most comprehensive sense, may be said to stand for the *significance* of the biblical message when it is heard as a witness to God.

In the first place, "promise" denotes the significance of cultic memory in the life of Israel. Moltmann, of course, does not deny that the Old Testament writings are composed of multifarious literary forms. The encounter between God and human beings is expressed in a rich variety of ways. The Hebrew vocabulary contains no single, exact equivalent of the Greek *epangelia*.[4] By "promise" he is not referring simply to selected texts or passages. His contention is rather that sacred memory functioned as promise in Hebrew faith; that is, it functioned as a pledge of Yahweh's encounter with Israel in that which was to come in the future. "The historical epiphanies of God, of which Israel could truly speak, were particular and transient epiphanies. Therefore, memory transforms them into signs and promises of the ultimate and eschatological epiphany of God at the end of history."[5] Tradition in the Old Testament perspective, as von Rad and his followers have emphasized, consisted less of rigid schematizations and formulations than of an ongoing process of interpretation. Elaborating upon this view of tradition, Moltmann writes, "Thus we find promise and history in a process of transformation in which the traditional passing on of the promises entered into the mastering of new experiences of history, and the new experiences of history were understood as transformations and explanations of the promises. Never, however, in this process of transformation was an understanding of history not opened up and bound up with promises."[6] The *significance* of this process of tradition, the *tradendum* which persisted in this dialectical transformation of sacred memory and historical experience, is what Moltmann characterizes as "promise."[7] Note that at this juncture we are introduced to the notion of a dialectical process which is drawn from Old Testament theology.

In the second place, the word "promise" is used by Moltmann to indicate the most fundamental significance of Jesus Christ in the New Testament writings. As we have noted, the resurrection is interpreted by Moltmann as an eschatological "setting-in-force" of the Abrahamic promise.[8] The variety of christological conceptions within the New Testament canon is not thereby denied, though Moltmann's interest as a systematic theologian is in locating unifying principles rather than in providing detailed exegeses of comparative texts. The aim in designating the key meaning of Jesus Christ as "promise" is not to impose one, uniform pattern upon all christological interpretations in the New Testament but to single out the decisive importance of the prevailing eschatological context in which each of these interpretations appears. The "apocalyptic" context of which Käsemann writes is what Moltmann has in mind when he, in agreement with Luther, describes the gospel as "promise." The presence of Christ in the faith of the early church involves the imminence of his parousia, regardless of the different ways in which this imminence is portrayed.

As reported in the New Testament, the resurrection of Jesus is not a concluded event which has become a datum of the past to be appropriated as archeological fact or as timeless myth. It is essentially the activation of a mission to all people which "necessitates" speech about Jesus as both crucified and risen.[9] Language is ingredient in the raising of Jesus from the dead. Proclamation is essential to the form of reality that the resurrection takes. To proclaim the resurrection is to signify by words and acts that the future of Jesus Christ brings with it the judgment and hope of every past and present. To proclaim the crucifixion is to signify that this future pertains not to some inner or otherworldly reality but precisely to those sufferings and injustices which exist in the same world that is marked by the sign *sub Pontio Pilato*. Thus the kerygmatic language-event of the New Testament exhibits a "contemporaneous noncontemporaneity" in that it generates in the present a mission which undermines the power of the present by witnessing to the pre-eminent power of the future.[10] The *missio* arises out of the *promissio*.[11] This correlation of *promissio* and *missio*, Moltmann argues, is the clue to the significance of the dialectic of *cross* and *resurrection* in the Christian Scriptures. Consequently, in this second instance he speaks of a dialectical process from the standpoint of New Testament theology.

There is yet a third sense in which Moltmann refers to promise as a language-event. Promise is the significance of the biblical message in the present day when it is heard as a witness to God. In this sense it is not restricted to an Old Testament or New Testament category. It is the term which most aptly denotes the kind of meaningfulness which the Christian gospel exhibits today in the community of faith. The mission of the Christian community in the contemporary world "bears in itself the character of promise."[12] The process of the tradition from Abraham to Christ and from the cross to the parousia continues.

When we inquire, therefore, into "the language of promise" we are inquiring at the most basic level into the significance of the biblical message for faith. The term denotes a mode of signification which Moltmann appropriates as the most essential hermeneutical category in the interpretation of Scripture and as the most viable unifying principle in dogmatics. To say more than this we must turn to the descriptions of promissory language-events which Moltmann offers.

THE FUNCTIONS OF PROMISSORY LANGUAGE

Let us examine now more closely what these language-events are said to do. We have already seen that Moltmann characterizes their logic by the term "hope-sentences." He approaches the problem of uncovering this logic by urging an analysis based not upon "the generic concept of species" but upon "the dynamic concept of function."[13] If we are to avoid appeals simply to "supernatural" knowledge in delineating the forces of promissory language, and if we are to refrain from positing arbitrary and unsupported claims with regard to their role in revelation, some other accounting must be given. What then are the functions of this promissory language?

First, taking into account the Old Testament background of the Word of God as promise, Moltmann employs a set of descriptions derived from Zimmerli.[14] He lists seven definitive marks of promise as an Old Testament conception. These he states as follows.

1. "A promise is an affirmation *(Zusage)* which announces a reality which is not yet."
2. "The promise binds man to the future and opens up to him a sense of history."
3. "The history which is determined and inaugurated by promise is not composed of cyclic recurrence but has a definite direction toward the promised and outstanding fulfillment."
4. "If the word is a word of promise this means that this word has not yet found its corresponding reality but that instead it stands in contradiction to present and formerly experienced reality. . . . 'Future,' moreover, means that reality in which the word of promise obtains its correspondence, its answer, and its fulfillment, in which it finds or creates a reality which conforms to it and in which it comes to rest."
5. "The word of promise always creates, therefore, an interval of a span of tension between the issuing and the redeeming of the promise."
6. "The promise is not abstracted from the promising God but rather its fulfillment is credited directly to the free faithfulness of God . . . (and not to) a fixed juridical system of historic necessities in a promise-fulfillment schema. . . ."
7. "The particular character of the Old Testament promises can be seen in the fact that the promises were not liquidated by the history of Israel—either through disappointments or through fulfillments—but rather they came to be known throughout Israel's experienced history in constantly new and expanding interpretations."

What Zimmerli presents as an account arrived at "through an investigation within the Old Testament" into "Old Testament forms"[15] Moltmann appropriates as systematic principles. These seven points are interpreted to apply not only to the role of Yahweh's words of covenant in shaping the life of ancient Israel, but also to the means of grace today. The "constantly new and expanding interpretations" of sacred memory as promise, referred to in point seven, continue in the ongoing Christian tradition, but the way in which memory operates in the community of faith remains essentially the same. That is the crucial insistence. As Moltmann expresses it, the promise "does not collapse with the historical circumstances and the historical thought forms in which it was received, but instead can transform itself—by interpretation—without losing its *character* of certainty, of expectation, and of movement."[16] It is this formal "character" of promissory significance which is at issue, and Moltmann's theory of revelation hinges upon the explication which he gives to it.

In this set of descriptions we can see that agency plainly is attributed to the promises in that they are said to do such things as "announce," "bind," "open up," "inaugurate," "obtain," and "create." As stated here in each case the word "promise" serves as the subject of a transitive verb. Within the framework of biblical thought, and of primitive religions generally, such statements are not unusual. In these contexts efficacy is commonly ascribed to the words of deity. But how are we to understand the efficacy of promissory language as a principle of systematic theology today?

Moltmann is quick to insist that the process set in motion by promise is not to be thought of as a natural or historical process constitutive of world reality as such. The eschaton is not to be identified with any organic *nisus* or *telos*. This is emphasized in point six. Nor is some promise-fulfillment scheme of *Heilsgeschichte* to be formulated which remains indifferent to critical historical science. Such philosophically anachronistic attempts on the part of theologians, Moltmann contends, merely throw a smokescreen over the very real crisis in which a theology of revelation finds itself in the modern world.[17] Steering a course between the Scylla of a naturalistic historicism and the Charybdis of a supernaturalistic theory of salvation-history, or between the inducements of a logical positivism, on the one hand, and of a revelational positivism, on the other, is no mean assignment for systematic theology. Yet Moltmann risks this very course in order to set forth a theory of how the language of promise is operative in revelation. "The decisive question," he writes, "is whether 'revelation' is the illuminating interpretation of an existing, obscure life process within history, or whether revelation itself sets the process of history going, propels it, and conducts it."[18]

In order to explain how the exegetical descriptions of promise as a biblical motif can be said to be applicable to an understanding of revelation today Moltmann draws upon a second source, this time a phenomenological study of "the experience of history" by Georg Picht.[19] The account which Moltmann provides of the functions of promissory language relies in large measure upon Picht. Moltmann makes seven explicit references to *Die Erfahrung der Geschichte*, but beyond these there are numerous parallels and correspondences between his ideas and Picht's which appear in additional instances in his writings where no citations are given.[20] These passages serve to confirm two conclusions: 1) Moltmann's concept of promise is nearly identical to Picht's concept of *time*, and 2) the recognition of this use of Picht enables us better to understand the controversial and sometimes apparently contradictory statements of Moltmann about "experience." This second point is especially pertinent to the American discussion of Moltmann's theology and will be taken up in the next chapter. We need only consider the first of these two observations here.

Picht acknowledges that his approach to the question of history is akin to, but not simply equatable with that of his teacher, Heidegger. We find in his discussion the same emphasis upon history as a "phenomenon" to be discovered within human experience, a phenomenon which is intrinsic to all experience and yet which generally remains hidden and unexpressed.[21] When Picht refers to "the experience of history" he tells us that he is speaking of a particular mode of experience in which the phenomenon of history comes to appearance and expression.

Time is the key concept which Picht examines. He observes that in Greek thought time images being by re-presenting the presence of that which remains unchanging and eternal. Only that which is constant and invariable may properly be said to be a subject of knowledge. Time is the mode in which the constant and invariable reality is brought into consciousness. With Kant we find a similar position, with this exception. Time, according to Kant, is the inner form of intuition, but it nevertheless continues to be conceived with reference to the idea of immutable "substance." Apart from unchanging "substance" time cannot be known. Substance is implicit in appearance as that which is constant and invariable amidst all alteration, a "pure identity and negation of all change."[22] Thus, Picht writes of Kant: "No longer is time the image of being, but rather substance is the image of time."[23]

What remains hidden and unrecognized in the Greek and Kantian interpretations of experience, Picht argues, is the fact that time itself is being. This statement means that "time" is the subject by which the predicate "being" is to be conceived. It is not "being," conceived along the lines of a Parmenidean ontology, which defines "time," so that one must think with the Greeks of time as imaging an eternally abiding reality, or think with Kant of time in reference to an eternally abiding substance. Rather, being is to be understood in terms of temporality. Time as it is experienced provides the clue to ontology.

The critique of the Parmenidean conception of the *logos* as an "epiphany of eternal presence," upon which so much of Moltmann's case depends, can be found in Picht. The following four illustrations suffice to demonstrate the parallelism of ideas and, in some cases, of exact wording between Picht's discussion and Moltmann's. In each instance note that the word "promise," as employed by Moltmann, may be substituted for the word "time," as employed by Picht, without substantially changing the predicate of the original sentence.

1. Picht: "Time itself is being."[24]
   Moltmann: "Promise itself is reality" and "cannot be separated as word from that reality which it announces."[25]
2. Picht: Time is not the "*repraesentatio*" of the past but the "*praesentatio* of the future."[26]
   Moltmann: "A promise announces a reality which has not yet arrived. But in announcing this future, the future becomes word-present. . . . The promise brings the future into the present in the word. . . ."[27]
3. Picht: "Time itself . . . makes room . . . for that which is not yet."[28]
   Moltmann: "The prospect [i.e., promise] of this future coming from God opens up . . . room for change and freedom."[29]
4. Picht: "It [i.e., time] does not set before us that which independently is already before us, but rather brings to the present what is not yet."[30]
   Moltmann: "Christian revelation [i.e., promise] does not set before us something which independently was already there before us . . . but rather brings to the present what is not yet, presents the future, and calls into being that which does not exist."[31]

In moving from exegesis to constructive theology Moltmann obviously borrows from the language and conceptuality of Picht. He does not, however, follow Picht and the Heideggerian viewpoint in the emphasis which they place upon the historicity of the *Dasein*.[32] The subject is changed from "time" to "promise," but the predicates remain the same. Moltmann has patterned his description of how the language of promise functions in large measure upon Picht's description of the existential dimensions of time.

There is yet a third factor in Moltmann's account of promissory significance which must not be overlooked. It is the use which he makes of the principles of "tendency" and "latency" in explaining the functions of promise. These concepts are employed in dialectical materialism to portray the historical process. Bloch is Moltmann's primary inspiration here. The link between possibility and actuality is not to be interpreted as "a causal necessity, but rather as the tendency *(Tendenz)*, the impulse *(Zug)*, the inclination *(Gefälle)*, the trend *(Trend)*, the definite propensities *(Neigungen)* for something which can become real in certain historic constellations." More exactly, " 'Tendency' means something which mediates between the real, objective possibilities and the subjective decision, and to that extent places the historical 'facts' in the stream of the historical process and the subjective decisions of the historical observer within the same process."[33] This "something" includes both language and happening. "The universals of the metaphysics of history are neither real nor solely verbal, but rather constitute tendencies in the potential."[34] Subjectivity and objectivity, possibility and actuality, existence and cosmos occur together in dialectical mediation within history. This Hegelian conception Moltmann carries over into his theory of revelation.

The task of uncovering the language of promise, and thereby of developing an eschatological understanding of revelation, thus becomes for Moltmann a matter of "lifting up the tendencies and latencies of the Christ event of the crucifixion and resurrection, and in seeking to estimate the possibilities opened up by this event."[35] The hiddenness of the world's future in the cross is the "latency" of the Christ event which is disclosed only in the "tendency" of the resurrection. The Reformation motif of grace hidden *sub contrario*, beneath its opposite, here is given a contemporary expression in Blochian categories. The dialectic of the cross and resurrection finds its final synthesis only in the eschaton. It is a dialectic open to the ultimate future and to the *novum* which has not yet taken place. ''The tendencies and latencies of the resurrection event are drawn out into the future opened up by it. With the raising of Jesus everything has not yet happened.''[36] To recognize that the vindication of Christ's will and way has not yet taken place in all things is to see that the glorification of God, the establishment of the kingdom, and the presence of eternal life in the defeat of death are still awaited and known to faith only in hope and anticipation. This future of God, which has been said to be already present in the form of promise, can now be depicted further as that which is latent in the death of Jesus. But this future is already present also in the tendency which the resurrection now exerts upon history, and this tendency must be included along with the latency of the cross in our understanding of promise.

These combined ideas of ''latency'' and ''tendency'' are used by Moltmann to support two conclusions. The first is that language and event, theory and practice, *promissio* and *missio* cannot be separated in a Christian view of revelation. The second is that the Cartesian dichotomy between the self and the world and the modern theological duality influenced by it between existential historicity and world history, or between sacred history and ordinary history, is overcome in a properly eschatological interpretation. Promissory logic provides a way to move beyond the impasse of personalist or existentialist reference, on the one hand, and cosmological reference, on the other, in accounting for the meaning and truth of theological claims. Self-understanding and world-understanding come together in a dialectical unity in the hearing and receiving of God's Word as promise. Moltmann sums up his position as follows: ''In developing the promises in the Christ event as latency and tendency we came upon a historic mediation of subject and object which permits us neither to classify the future of Christ within a system of sacred history and world history . . . nor to reflect on the future of Christ within the existential futurity of man.''[37] The language of promise functions in such a way that subjectivity and objectivity both may be maintained in their interconnection.

Finally, let us take note of the function of negation which Moltmann ascribes to promise. In considering the topic of hope-sentences we have observed that in anticipating, initiating, and presenting the future, promises are said to contradict the present. Once again the explanation of this process is couched in a framework of thought adapted from Hegelian concepts. Moltmann clearly does not wish to minimize the value of cultural achievement. His argument is that such value is to be judged in terms of its openness to the future. This is implicit in the thesis that memory functions as promise. There are tendencies of hope in the past. But these tendencies move toward their historical realization only by presently negating that which seeks to foreclose the future. "Everything past can be understood as future begun or as future aborted."[38] Moltmann explains, "To give further theoretical expression to this line of thinking, one might say that the anticipations and analogies of the future become manifest in present reality through the historical dialectic of the negation of the negative. The dialectic of thesis and antithesis is the presupposition by which one can recognize in the thesis the prefiguration of the future synthesis."[39] The latency of the cross becomes known only insofar as the tendency of the resurrection works to undermine all that stands in opposition to this latency. That is why the content of the promises must be defined negatively; what is promised is the negation of those powers which presently negate the fulfillment of God's will, *viz.*, sin, suffering, and death. "The positive is always represented by the negation of the negative."[40] This is the dialectical structure of the process by which the language of promise creates the experience of history.

In appropriating for contemporary theology a conception first suggested by Old Testament interpreters, Moltmann has thus found it necessary to set forth a theory of how the language of promise may be understood to be operative today in revelation. Selected themes from Zimmerli, Picht, and Bloch are woven together in an attempt to explain the efficacy of promissory language-events. The fabric of the argument remains to be tested. The move from scriptural exegesis to systematic theology, in Moltmann's view, requires that "Christian theology . . . think and speak, question and answer within the arena of present day philosophy."[41] Conceptual problems cannot be avoided. Theories do not consist of axiomatic truth-statements. How adequate, then, in terms of his own standards, is Moltmann's explanation of the functions of promises?

PROBLEMS IN MOLTMANN'S THEORY

To follow Moltmann's own criteria of evaluation we must ask about both the exegetical foundation of his position and the systematic interpretation which he offers as a contemporary theological understanding. While our primary concern is with the systematic questions, we cannot avoid inquiring if Moltmann's first condition for the making of Christian theological claims has been met. Is this theory of the language of promise one that is governed by Scripture? Is it sufficiently grounded in biblical theology?

These questions obviously apply an imprecise standard. The issue of whether or not a theological position is congruent with Scripture submits to no simple resolution.[42] What Moltmann's first criterion actually means is that an exegetical case must be made for any proposal dealing with the loci of Christian doctrine.[43] It clearly rejects what the Reformers called "speculative theology," and it requires that the systematic theologian be responsible both for deciding among often differing exegetical possibilities, and for accounting for these decisions in light of continuing biblical scholarship. Moltmann does provide such a case. His concentration upon promise as a key to the systematic unity of the biblical witness does have a basis, as we have noted, in the work of certain contemporary biblical theologians.[44] Nevertheless, the exegetical foundations of any theology remain open to question and further insight.[45]

Moltmann's account of promise, while substantially influenced by biblical theology, is itself a theoretical proposal and must be treated as such. There is no "language of promise" as text which can be uncovered solely by exegesis. If by this term we are to think of a form of *significance*, that is, if the word "promise" is being used to refer to the *meaning (Bedeutung)* of the revelatory event, as Moltmann says,[46] then we are confronted here not only with a matter of exegesis but with a matter of logic. It would be mistaken to suppose that it is within the purview of exegetical research alone to determine what this promissory logic is.[47]

We may best pursue this point by turning attention to four problems which inhere in Moltmann's theory.

1. The first has to do with the initial assumption itself that revelation as a language-event exhibits a form of meaning which can be "un-

covered." Moltmann's theory is inconsistent on the question of whether this promissory logic is intrinsic to the reality of revelation. This inconsistency may be traced to an attempt to revise Barth while at the same time maintaining certain Barthian premises.

The contrast between Moltmann's position and that of Barth on this issue is at once subtle and decisive. In their basic approach and outlook they would appear to be in general agreement. Both positions hold that the initiative in revelation belongs solely with God, that this revelation is to be thought of as the language or speech of God communicated to human beings, and that this language involves always an act or an event.[48] Barth also characterizes this act as one which creates history. "The Word of God in the highest sense makes history."[49] Furthermore, for Barth, as well as for Moltmann, the language-event in which revelation occurs is ordinary human language. This point should be underscored in order to keep in mind that the difference between their positions does not lie here. In opposition to Tillich, for example, Barth argues that the statement "God speaks" is not to be understood merely "symbolically" in a manner "totally foreign to the meaning of this proposition."[50] "The concepts act and mystery cannot, therefore, because they are necessarily explanatory, point us away from the concept of speech or language, but because they are explanations can only point us back repeatedly to it as the original text. . . . We hasten to add that also there is no Word of God without a physical event."[51] Barth, thus, does not refer to "language" in some otherworldly, non-linguistic sense, but in the sense in which ordinary words of human speech are found in church proclamation, in Scripture, and in the humanity of Jesus Christ himself.

The disagreement between Barth and Moltmann in this area arises instead over the fact that in Barth's view the ordinary linguistic forms in which revelation occurs, the words by which the Word is spoken, are said to contribute nothing as such to the significance of revelation. When God chooses to speak through human language the "logical form" of this discourse discloses nothing with respect to revelation.[52] As Barth explains it, "The form of the Word of God is therefore really that of the cosmos which stands in contradiction to God. It as little has in it the capacity of revealing God to us as we on our part have the capacity for knowing God in it. If God's Word is manifest in it, it happens, of course, 'through it,' but in such a way that this 'through it' means 'in spite of it.' ''[53] This "through" and yet "in spite of" characteristic accompanies every physical event in which God speaks. The "logical form" of revelatory language is not intrinsic to the revelation.

As Barth develops his doctrine of the relation of the Word of God to ordinary language he distinguishes between what he calls the "spiritual" and the "physical," or "natural," senses of this language. "The Word of God has also natural power, but primarily and preeminently and decisively the simple spiritual power of truth. What we here assert of the Word of God does not hold equally of every word. . . . For any other word physis signifies its limit, at which the lack of power in its spirituality is simultaneously exposed."[54] This view is to be recognized as a corollary of Barth's central thesis that God in his freedom distinguishes himself from creation precisely in the very act of relating himself to creation in self-disclosure by the miracle of grace. The event of revelation thus imposes a "spiritual" significance upon the "physical" medium of natural speech which this medium, since it shares in the fallenness of all things human, does not intrinsically possess. Barth uses this interpretation of the significance of revelatory language to elucidate his claim that neither the cosmos nor the self, in either its capacities or its incapacities, has any inherent power to make the revelation of God happen. There are no cosmological or anthropological structures which in themselves disclose, or afford the possibility that investigation may disclose, the Creator's gracious and eventful relationship to creation. In revelation it is what happens in the "spiritual sphere" which creates its proper analogies in the "natural sphere" and not vice versa.[55]

By arguing that a form of logical significance, i.e., promise as a language-event, is essential and not merely adventitious to the reality of revelation, and further by operating on the premise that this significance can be described with regard to its functions, Moltmann, in effect, breaks decisively with Barth on the question of the relation of the words to the Word. His position cannot be maintained within the framework of Barth's distinction between "physical" ("natural") and "spiritual" significance. It becomes self-contradictory to say that revelation occurs "in spite of" its creaturely form, or that the "logical form'' of revelatory language contributes nothing as such to the significance of this language for faith.

According to Barth, the linguistic form of the Word of God is dialectically contradicted by the Word, conceived as the *Deus praesens*. According to Moltmann, the linguistic form of the Word of God is not contradicted but confirmed by the Word, conceived as the *Deus adventus*. The contradiction brought about by revelation is to be seen, not as the inadequacy of any human form of speech in itself to correspond to God's present reality, but as the inadequacy of any present state of reality to correspond to God's presence as promised. The promissory form of revelatory language remains essential in this understanding.

But it is precisely at this point that Moltmann's position becomes equivocal. The implications of such a revision of Barth are not acknowledged. Instead, while contending, as Barth would not, for a functional analysis of what the language of promise does, Moltmann nevertheless seeks to maintain with Barth that the process by which the Word of God makes history cannot be reduced to any abstract or necessarily fixed scheme of promise and fulfillment.[56] Logical necessity would seem to be excluded here as contrary to God's freedom. What then can be meant by the formal "character" of revelatory language which a functional analysis is supposed to uncover? Barth's often repeated denial of any applicability to divine reality of so-called "general conceptions" drawn from human phenomena is undoubtedly in the background here.[57] As a result Moltmann's argument vacillates on the one question which would appear to be crucial to his whole undertaking; namely, what, if anything, does the logical form of human promises have to tell us about the promises of God?

2. A second problem arises in Moltmann's attempt to characterize the relation of the words of revelation to the Word, to God. In rejecting the Barthian notion that the words in their "spiritual" efficacy unveil the eternal presence of God, that the ordinary language-events of proclamation are thus brought into correspondence with the divine selfhood, Moltmann is bound also to reject the notion that the language of revelation functions essentially as a *reference* to deity. The Anselmian presupposition that a correlation obtains in faith between the noetic and the ontic, between our ideas of God and the being of God, which is

at the basis of Barth's doctrine, is elaborated by Barth to include the assumption that the meaning of a word lies in its capacity to refer beyond itself.[58] "But when we do take the humanity of the Bible quite seriously, we must also take quite definitely the fact that as a human word it does say something specific, that as a human word it points away from itself, that as a word it points towards a fact *(Sache)*, an object *(Gegenstand)*. In this respect, too, it is a genuine human word. What human word is there which does not do the same?"[59] Moltmann's view, in contrast to Barth, as we have observed, is that in the eschatological context of the biblical traditions no transcendental selfhood is revealed. Instead, there is revealed the continuing faithfulness of God as the keeper of his word in history. It is this shift from a conception of divine transcendental unity *(Ichheit)* to a conception of divine historical constancy *(Selbigkeit)* which discloses the inadequacy of the referential presupposition regarding revelatory language. The significance of promises cannot be explained sufficiently by the theory that words exist primarily as pointers to facts and objects beyond themselves.

Yet here Moltmann's theory confronts a dilemma. If the words of revelation are not to be understood primarily as referring to God, if reference is not their sole or even dominant function, then are we left with the position that revelation provides only an inferential knowledge of God? Is *inference* the only alternative to *reference* in accounting for the role of language in revelation?

This question is posed, but not resolved, by the fraternal debate between Moltmann and Pannenberg. Moltmann objects to Pannenberg's proposal of a doctrine of the indirect self-revelation of God in history as a corrective for the Barthian doctrine of a direct self-revelation of God in word.[60] This alternative, in Moltmann's judgment, amounts to a return to the Greek mode of cosmological reasoning concerning deity. *Eschaton* has supplanted *arche* as the source of revelation in the cosmos, but in each case the "inference-process" *(Ruckschlussverfahrens)* is the same. Pannenberg, for his part, disclaims any identification of his position with that of the classical cosmological argument, but proceeds to level the following charge against Moltmann. "This dispute should not cause us to forget that all thought, insofar as it combines propositions, moves in inferences. It would lead to a laughable self-deception if one tried to exclude reasoning from knowledge of God altogether. And as far as the inference is concerned, the 'recognition of the identity of God from promise to fulfillment,' which Moltmann . . . 'opposes to the inference from the effect to the cause,' this itself has the same logical structure as an inference.''[61]

The issue, then, is how one is to arrive at an understanding of God as subject from the words of revelation. Is there a logical structure to promissory language itself which involves something other than the categories of reference and inference? Moltmann's theory requires that further consideration be given to this question.

3. The third problem is that the conceptions of "the future" *(die Zukunft* or *Adventus)* and "the new" *(das Novum)* which Moltmann incorporates into his theory are incompatible with his conception of promise as a language-event. The warrant for these ontological categories is not provided by any linguistic evidence. They have not been uncovered from an examination of the language of promise but have been taken over with certain modifications from a philosophy of dialectical world-process in which promise has no central place. The result is that some of the things originally said about "promise," namely, how the promise functions, are later said about "the future" and "the new." But these terms cannot logically be equated. It is one thing to say that a promise creates a new state of affairs. It is quite another to say that the future does so. The former is speech which provides us with a subject-matter. The latter is an abstract idea which does not. We shall look more directly at the ontological dimensions of Moltmann's proposal in Chapter V. Here it is necessary only to point out how the claims which are made for "the future" and "the new" conflict with the claims which are made for promissory language.

We are told initially that revelation in the mode of promise is to be understood, to cite a typical summary statement, as a *"primum movens* at the head of the historical process,'' a prime mover which "points forwards and leads forwards.''[62] Agency is located firmly within the language-event as that which "creates" the future in which the promise finds its realization.[63] The promise is portrayed as neither a "prophecy" concerning God,[64] nor as a "providence" at once decreed by and yet distinguishable from God,[65] but as itself being of the reality of God and essential to that future which it alone announces and generates.

However, as Moltmann elaborates his position he draws increasingly upon the Blochian notion that "the real genesis is not at the beginning but at the end,"[66] and the creative efficacy initially ascribed to promissory language is now ascribed to the future itself as "the mode of God's being."[67] "The future" and "the new" which the words of promise were originally said to create now are given ontological status in their own right as efficacious forces, and the promise is interpreted merely as one of the forms of anticipatory consciousness delineated by Bloch in the order of daydreams and wishes. In discussing the category of *das Novum* Moltmann writes, "But, in fact, the new is never wholly new. It is always preceded by a dream, a promise, an anticipation; otherwise we could not grasp and accept it, and it could not be *effective* in history."[68] This is a Blochian doctrine. The "effective" character of the promise is still affirmed, but it now is explained according to Bloch's theory of anticipation without regard to any empirical reality of the promise as language and to the difference between the promise as a language-event and such other forms of anticipations as wishes and dreams. By such a procedure the aim of developing a doctrine of the revelation of God by "uncovering the language of promise" is in actual practice abandoned.

4. Finally, it is apparent as an overall problem that in proceeding to uncover the language of promise Moltmann has resorted to conceptions which clearly are not derived from linguistic evidence. As we have seen with regard to the borrowings from both Picht and Bloch, ontological categories rather than descriptions based upon an examination of language are applied to the promises. This gives his discussion of the functions of promissory language the very arbitrariness which by declared intent he seeks to avoid.

On the one hand, the characterization of promise is drawn in terms of an anti-logos. This approach rests upon an alleged dichotomy between Greek and Hebrew ways of thinking which has itself increasingly been viewed as problematical in recent biblical scholarship.[69] On the other hand, dialectical patterns of interpretation rather than empirical investigation determine what is said about the promises.[70] Because of both of these factors almost no attention, surprisingly enough, is given to promising as a speech-act in everyday discourse. The significance of ordinary language for the language of revelation remains unexplored.

With these problems before us I wish now to extend the boundaries of this discussion somewhat by turning to a brief consideration of the characteristics of promises as they have been analyzed by ordinary language philosophers. We will then be in a position to determine the extent to which these studies may be of relevant value in the theological attempt to develop an understanding of the form of revelation as a promissory language-event.

PROMISE AS A SPEECH-ACT IN
ORDINARY DISCOURSE

I refer particularly to the investigation of promising as a "speech-act" as it is undertaken in the writings of J. L. Austin, Donald Evans, and John Searle. Let us look at the findings of each in turn.

Contemporary philosophical interest in promising as a speech-act is primarily indebted to the work of Austin. Austin's own efforts in this regard were no doubt in part stimulated by H. A. Prichard, his teacher and predecessor as White's professor of moral philosophy at Oxford. Prichard labored to understand the relation between the making of a promise and the duty of keeping it, a duty which he believed to be clearly presupposed in promise-making but, just as self-evidently, not produced thereby. "We get into difficulties, however," he acknowledged, "as soon as we try to state what that is in what we call making a promise the production of which renders us bound to do the action which we are said to promise to do."[71] Prichard's rather opaque conclusion, which he proffered "only with the greatest hesitation," was that promising can only occur among parties who are in effect bound by "an agreement not to use certain noises except in a certain way."[72] In retrospect it appears that this conclusion prefigured the direction which Austin's later, more exacting research was to take.[73]

Austin's inquiry into the "certain noises" which are used in a "certain way" in the case of promising led to the notion which has now widely come to be associated with his name, *performative utterance*.[74] His philosophy consists in large measure of continued refinements and revisions of this basic linguistic category. We see the emergence of this conception in an early essay, "Other Minds" (1946), where Austin launches a critique of the "descriptive fallacy," the assumption that meaningful speech functions primarily to describe. "Even if some language is now purely descriptive," he writes, "language was not in origin so, and much of it is still not so. Utterance of obvious ritual phrases, in the appropriate circumstances, is not *describing* the action we are doing, but *doing* it. . . . Such phrases cannot, strictly, *be* lies, though they can 'imply' lies, as 'I promise' implies that I fully intend, which may be untrue."[75] The language used in making a promise does not serve simply to inform the hearer that a promise has been made. The speaking *is* the promising, and thus to say "I promise you" is to do something quite different from what is done in saying "I promised you" or "he promises you." The latter two instances are examples of true or false statements. The former instance is not. There is a distinction to be observed between the informative and performative aspects of speech.

It is this distinction which Austin develops in his later essay, "Performative Utterances" (1956). Here he offers an initial definition of a "performative" as "a kind of utterance which looks like a statement and grammatically . . . would be classed as a statement, which is not nonsensical, and yet is not true or false."[76] Promising again is singled out as a paradigm of such an utterance. A promise is not properly characterized as a reference to a commitment; it is the commitment itself. Unlike statements which refer to or report on independently existing states of affairs promises must be said to institute states of affairs. Austin writes, "The one thing we must not suppose is that what is needed in addition to the saying of the words in such cases is the performance of some internal spiritual act, of which the words then are to be the report. . . . In the case of promising—for example, 'I promise to be there tomorrow'—it's very easy to think that the utterance is simply the outward and visible (that is, verbal) sign of the performance of some inward spiritual act of promising, and this view has certainly been expressed in many classic places."[77] As far as the explicit act of promising itself is concerned the distinction between referend and referent, or between sign and reality, does not apply.

Although performatives are not reducible simply to true or false statements they are, Austin points out, rule governed forms of language. There are conventions of speech which cannot be violated if the performative is to occur. The appropriate conditions for performing a particular speech-act must be present. Austin terms a failure to meet these conditions an *infelicity*. It is the task of linguistic analysis to uncover these conventions and conditions and thereby specify what infelicities are possible. One cannot say, for example, that a promise, in any generally understood meaning of that word, has been made unless certain procedures intrinsic to the making of promises have been observed. The form of promissory language is thus integral to its content. With uncharacteristic hyperbole Austin remarks that with the discovery of "performative utterance" and "infelicities" we are provided with "two shining new tools to crack the rib of reality maybe" and "two shining new skids under our metaphysical feet."[78]

Continued examination discloses, however, as Austin goes on to acknowledge, that the distinction between performative and descriptive statements is neither clear-cut nor absolute. To illustrate, how is one to classify the utterance, "I am sorry"?[79] Is it exclusively a description of an inner state, exclusively an act of apology, or are both these elements present? Furthermore, while some linguistic expressions are *explicitly performative,* namely, those which have a first person, indicative mood, active voice, present tense grammatical structure, others are nevertheless implicitly so but may not be recognized as such. Infelicities, it can be shown, may occur in the making of statements as well as in the making of explicit performatives. This recognition leads Austin to revise his initial definition and to speak of performatives not as a separate class of utterances but as distinguishable *forces of utterances.* In uncovering the significance of any speech-act, therefore, one must inquire not only into its propositional content but into its force.[80] These then are the four linguistic classifications which Austin introduces in the essay "Performative Utterances": the performative, the infelicity, the explicit performative, and the forces of utterances.

Austin explains these points even further in his William James Lectures at Harvard in 1955.[81] Here we have the most detailed explication of his views. More precise classifications are ventured, reformulated, and tested in the course of these lectures. There is a refreshing if sometimes exasperating lack of finality about all of Austin's conclusions. Yet the essential insights persist amidst his constant search for more exact distinctions. Not all of his points need concern us here. What should be observed is that the original contrast between performatives and statements (or to use the term Austin comes to prefer, "constatives") is once again shown to be only partially apt. It is more accurate to say that all speaking involves the performance of acts. What is important from a logical viewpoint is to delineate the types of acts which are performed. Austin distinguishes three such types.[82] The *locutionary act* is the act of saying something, of uttering a sentence that makes sense in the language. The *illocutionary act* is the way in which a locution is used. "It may be perfectly clear what I mean by 'It is going to charge' or 'Shut the door,' but not clear whether it is meant as a statement or warning, etc."[83] In addition to the act *of* saying something the speaker performs an act *in* saying something. Every locution exhibits some illocutionary force if the context in which the speaking occurs, the total speech-act, is taken into account. In the third place, it is apparent that in performing locutionary and illocutionary acts a speaker may also intentionally produce an effect or result through his utterance. This act Austin labels *perlocutionary*. The performance in this instance is not, as in the case of a locution, an act *of* saying something, and not, as in the case of an illocution, an act which occurs *in* saying something, but rather it is an act which occurs *by* saying something. Unlike the illocutionary force of an utterance with which it is most liable to be confused, and which also may properly be said to take effect, perlocutionary consequences are not achieved by means of linguistic conventions. In this respect they are not rule governed.

Of these three types of acts it is the illocutionary which exhibits what Austin in the beginning designated simply as performative force and which interests him the most. There are, he suggests, five more or less clearly definable classes of these illocutionary forces to which the following labels may be applied.[84] *Verdictives* are utterances which in addition to their propositional content render a judgment, a ruling, a verdict. *Exercitives* are a means of exerting powers, as in such speech-acts as ordaining, charging, bequeathing, etc. *Commissives* are of special interest for our purposes because they are, Austin explains, "typified by promising." He writes, "They *commit* you to doing something, but include also declarations or announcements of intention, which are not promises, and also rather vague things which we may call espousals, as, for example, siding with. They have obvious connections with verdictives and exercitives."[85] *Behabitives* are responses to behavior, either past or potential, which indicate the attitude of the speaker toward this behavior. Instances are apologizing, thanking, sympathizing, etc. *Expositives,* the fifth classification, indicate how a speaker is presenting, or expositing, his views. Austin offers here the examples of stating, describing, answering, affirming, conceding, testifying, and the like. He writes, "To sum up, we may say that the verdictive is an exercise of judgment, the exercitive is an assertion of influence or exercising of power, the commissive is an assuming of an obligation or declaring of an intention, the behabitive is the adopting of an attitude, and the expositive is the clarifying of reasons, arguments, and communications."[86] Of these designations Austin admits that the last two are more indefinite than the others and require further scrutiny. Yet with the recognition of the illocutionary forces of speech-acts and of the felicitous uses of linguistic conventions which they entail the discussion is considerably advanced beyond Prichard's tentative insight that the act of promising presupposes an implicitly agreed to condition that "certain noises" be used in a "certain way."

Building upon Austin's analysis and extending it still further Donald Evans has brought these findings to bear upon the theological task of providing a contemporary understanding of the efficacy which biblical faith confesses to find in divine language.[87] Evans's work therefore speaks directly to our subject. "This biblical conception of language as an activity, of words as dynamic instruments," he writes, "is alien to philosophies in which words are only used to express inner thoughts or to state facts. Modern analytical philosophy helps to make the biblical conception seem less alien."[88] If present day theologies of the Word are to avoid the charge that they are merely positing arbitrary claims they would do better, Evans suggests, to look for supporting reasons in the "contemporary philosopher's analysis of everyday speech in any language" than in the "alleged peculiarities of the Hebrew language."[89] While such analyses do not enable us to appropriate meaningfully all of the "magical" powers commonly ascribed to words in ancient times, they do permit us to see that in the biblical perspective "the efficacious word of God in Creation has not only supernatural causal power but also Exercitive, Verdictive, and Commissive force."[90] This recognition, in Evans's judgment, provides a new basis for understanding how God's word may be said to exert certain definable powers which do not require supernaturalistic explanation. It opens up the possibility of a "new logic" for theology.[91] We have seen that the term "promise" for Moltmann in its most comprehensive sense designates the kind of meaning or significance which the biblical message has when it is received in faith. Evans, for his part, depicts the posture of faith as one in which the believer indicates by his response that he "looks on" the biblical message as a performative act. The believer takes the scriptural witness to God's word to be God's word to him. His faith stance is an *onlook*[92] which as such carries with it evident logical entailments, and his response exhibits the describable characteristics of a *correlative performative*.[93] If we interpret Moltmann's claim with the use of Evans's insights we can translate that claim as follows. To say that the biblical message has a particular significance for faith is to say that faith, whatever else it may be, is an "onlook" which receives the scriptural witness in a certain way. To say that this particular significance is promissory is to add that this onlook is a correlative response to commissive force. To say that the biblical message exhibits commissive force is to acknowledge that revelatory language is *self-involving*. This is Evans's major point. The logic of a commissive performative discloses a dimension of irreducible self-involvement.[94] Evans's primary contribution to the uncovering of the language of promise in ordinary discourse is his recognition of the self-involving character of this language and its implications for the logic of theological discourse.

Thus to the analytical tools which Austin provides we may now add Evans's concepts of *onlooks, correlative performatives,* and *self-involving utterance.*

We have yet to see precisely what factors constitute the issuance of a promise in ordinary discourse. What are the essential conditions comprising such a speech-act? Our third resource, John Searle, distinguishes nine such conditions and from these establishes five semantical rules governing the illocutionary force of promises.[95] By taking account of the results of Searle's investigation into everyday language we will be in a position to determine the extent to which divine promising as a linguistic occurrence may be said to carry the same logical entailments as human promising. Searle's list of conditions for felicitous or "nondefective" promising contains these points.[96]

1. *Normal input and output conditions obtain.* This stipulation

assures that there are no hindrances to the intelligibility of the speech on the part of either the speaker or the hearer. It applies to all illocutionary acts and not only to promising.

2. *In promising the speaker expresses a proposition in the utterance of a sentence.* The proposition is, however, only one aspect of the total speech-act. In addition to the proposition there is also the aspect of illocutionary force.

3. *In expressing a promise the speaker predicates a future act on his part.* One does not, strictly speaking, promise that he has previously done something but that he will do something. Nor does one promise that someone else will do something, but only that he intends to see that someone else does something.

4. *The hearer would prefer the speaker's doing this act to his not doing it, and the speaker believes that the hearer would prefer his doing the act to his not doing it.* Searle here distinguishes promises from threats, warnings, and from emphatic assertions or denials which take the form "I promise you that I did (or didn't)" in response to an accusation concerning a past act.

5. *It is not already obvious to both the speaker and the hearer that the speaker will do the act in the normal course of events.* One does not promise to do what is plainly already being done anyway.

6. *The speaker intends to do the action.* This point Searle designates as the condition of sincerity.

7. *The speaker intends that the utterance of the sentence will place him under an obligation to do the act.* Here we are back with Prichard's problem. The intentional undertaking of an obligation is essential to the act of promising and distinguishes the force of this act from that of other illocutions. If this intention is not present the promise is defective.

8. *The speaker intends to produce in the hearer the knowledge that the utterance of the sentence is to count as placing the speaker under an obligation to do the action. The speaker intends to produce this knowledge by means of the recognition of his intention, and he intends for his intention to be recognized in virtue of (by means of) the hearer's knowledge of the meaning of the sentence.* Thus we have an answer to Prichard's problem which is yet a further explication of Prichard's original insight that in promising it is presupposed that "certain

noises" are being used in a "certain way." Searle writes, "In this case the speaker assumes that the semantic rules (which determine the meaning) of the expressions uttered are such that the utterance counts as the undertaking of an obligation."[97] This condition poses the task of discovering what exactly these rules are.

9. *The semantical rules of the dialect spoken by the speaker and the hearer are such that the sentence is correctly and sincerely uttered if and only if conditions 1–8 obtain.* The sentence must be one which the speaker by personal intention and linguistic convention employs for the making of a promise.

From these nine conditions Searle derives the following five rules of semantics for determining which indicators of illocutionary force qualify as promissory. He writes as follows:[98]

> The semantical rules for the use of any illocutionary force indicating device Pr for promising are:
> *Rule* 1. Pr is to be uttered only in the context of a sentence (or larger stretch of discourse) *T,* the utterance of which predicates some future act *A* of the speaker *S.* I call this the *propositional content rule.* It is derived from the propositional content conditions 2 and 3.
> *Rule* 2. Pr is to be uttered only if the hearer *H* would prefer *S*'s doing *A* to his not doing *A,* and *S* believes *H* would prefer *S*'s doing *A* to his not doing *A.*
> *Rule* 3. Pr is to be uttered only if it is not obvious to both *S* and *H* that *S* will do *A* in the normal course of events. I call rules 2 and 3 *preparatory rules,* and they are derived from the preparatory conditions 4 and 5.
> *Rule* 4. Pr is to be uttered only if *S* intends to do *A.* I call this the *sincerity rule,* and it is derived from the sincerity condition 6.
> *Rule* 5. The utterance of *Pr* counts as the undertaking of an obligation to do *A.* I call this the *essential rule.*

These then are the rules which comprise the human institution of promising. As such they represent what Searle defines as "institutional facts."[99] They arise from the ways of human speech but are for this reason no less factual than the "brute facts" of empirical observation appealed to in the natural sciences. Their delineation is subject to detection and confirmation and is not simply arbitrary. Hence, as Austin earlier saw, promises involve definite conventions as well as intentions, and both are specifiable. As illocutionary speech-acts they display not only a *content* (the proposition) but also a *function* (the illocutionary force as depicted in these rules with which the proposition is expressed), and the one cannot be divorced from the other.[100] To talk, therefore, of the functional significance of promissory language in this context is not to subscribe to the facile and false position that meaning is simply use.[101] Rather, the situation when analysed is at once richer and more complex than this. As Searle concludes, "Speaking a language . . . consists of performing speech acts according to rules, and there is no separating those speech acts from the commitments" [Evans would say "self-involvement"] "which form essential parts of them."[102] We cannot understand the significance of promise as a speech-act if we fail to recognize these institutional facts. Must the same be said of the theological significance of promise as a revelatory language-event?

Returning now to the subject before us, our next step is to ask how these findings of Austin, Evans, and Searle assist us in dealing with the problems which we have encountered in Moltmann's theory of the language of promise.

THE LOGIC OF PROMISE

Let us look again at each of the four problems which Moltmann's theory presents in light of these analytical investigations of promissory speech-acts.

1. Implications of the claim that the form of revelation is promissory.

What the linguistic philosophies of Austin, Evans, and Searle make plain is that the natural significance of ordinary language involves, at a minimum, more than Barth is willing to grant. Such language, if one is serious in affirming its place in revelation, as both Barth and Moltmann claim to be, cannot be reduced to mere words which are somehow divested of their performative forces as speech-acts. To say that divine revelation occurs by way of ordinary language, whatever else may be involved, is to allow that logical forces are necessarily part of the signification situation.[103] To deny this is to make all talk of "language" in the usual sense of the word meaningless.

Furthermore, with respect to Moltmann's position, once the distinction between naming and promising is acknowledged as crucial for a proper understanding of revelatory language, the logical difference between these two acts must be demonstrated. The distinction cannot, according to Moltmann's own standards, simply be posited without supporting evidence. But the contrasts which Moltmann draws between "descriptive sentences" and "hope sentences," or between "description words" and "action words," are insufficient to provide this demonstration. As proffered characterizations of language they remain elemental and undeveloped. This becomes most apparent when the work of the linguistic philosophers is taken into consideration. One does not have to commit oneself to any predetermined set of conclusions to recognize the pertinence to a theory of revelation as promise of such questions as, What conditions constitute a promissory act? What self-involvements do such acts entail? What effects of promising are rule-governed and can be logically delineated (illocutionary)? What effects are not rule-governed and cannot be logically delineated (perlocutionary)? A theory which addresses such questions, as any other theory, obviously will not make revelation happen or produce faith in God. That is not the purpose of a theory in theology. It will, in a much more restricted but not unimportant sense, make understandable at least the claim that if revelatory language is promissory it carries certain initiatory forces which are not reducible simply to the forces of descriptive statements.

2. God known as subject from the words of promise.

More specifically, we have encountered in the logic of commissive force an irreducible element of the promisor's "self-involvement." This recognition relates to the second problem in Moltmann's theory. It enables us to account for the meaning of the following claims, each of which Moltmann is intent to affirm, without recourse to a logic of reference or to a logic of inference, both of which he finds to be inadequate.

First, God is revealed in promissory language as a promising subject. Promising, that is to say, carries with it the notion of agency. Second, this agency, if promissory, is personal and cannot be objectified as some impersonal causal mechanism. The objectivity of God is to be understood as that of a promisor's active commitment to others in the present for a future. Third, as promisor the subject of revelation includes both a "who" and a "what." Revelation discloses both self-involvement and propositional content, that is, both a thou and a coming kingdom, both a "someone" and a "something."[104] The who and the what of revelation cannot be understood apart from *how* revelation occurs.[105] Fourth, the promissory character of revelation, the how factor, nevertheless is not to be thought of as some logical a priori which as such has power to disclose the who-ness or the what-ness of God. The propositional content of a promise is not to be confused with its illocutionary force. What the logic of self-involvement enables us to understand is the claim that in revelation the believer encounters God as a committed subject. No logic can reveal *who* this subject is or *what* the content of these commitments are. Fifth, the kind of relationship which revelation establishes between God as promisor and the believer, the kind of knowing afforded to faith, is of the order of a "correlative performative." It is never a mere theoretical cognizance, but self-involving trust. This explains why all ideas of the knowledge of God based upon an indirect process of inferential reasoning prove unsatisfactory.[106]

Nevertheless, in considering these five points we must ask if the words and actions of human beings in proclaiming the gospel can rightfully be treated as *God's* "speech-act." Do we not run adrift here on the inevitable divide between things human and things divine? Is it more accurately the case that all human testimony of God is but a report, a statement, concerning a putative promise and thus not itself analyzable as a commissive performative with a self-involving dimension?[107]

To answer we must recognize that the human proclamation of God's promise is neither a human belief-utterance nor a human report of a divine promise. It is the medium in which God's own act of promising may intelligibly be said to occur. Whether "God" indeed does so act can only be proven in forthcoming events. But is not such the case with any promise? One must take another at the other's word. At the issuance of a promise no recipient can demonstrate the sincere intention of a promisor. Only a promisor can do that—and only in events which are to come. Faith is present whenever the proclamation of the gospel is heard as God's first person, present indicative promise to us. The self-involvement which is evidenced in proclamation insofar as it becomes for faith a commissive speech-act is never dependent upon or equatable with the involvement or lack of involvement of any human speaker.

3. Promissory language and the future.

We come now, in the third instance, to the problem of the incompatibility of the conceptions which Moltmann employs in moving from exegesis or biblical theology to dogmatics. What is required is an interpretation without internal contradiction of the relation of the language of promise to the new reality of the future. Do these linguistic characterizations which have been given of promise as a speech-act afford a more coherent way of conceiving the dynamics of revelation and at the same time do justice to such factors as continuity, newness, and the element of incongruity with present states of affairs which Moltmann is intent to affirm?

To answer this question we must begin where Moltmann himself begins with the presupposition that the reality of God can only be known in terms of the Word of God. More precisely, the dynamic by which revelation creates a new state of affairs must be one which has its locus in promissory language. Otherwise the linguistic and historical character of revelation is denied, and the kind of ahistorical transcendentalism which Barth is criticized for representing is reinstituted. By remaining with the word-character of revelation one is also forced to reject all ontological categories of an immanent world process. Such categories are not consonant with Moltmann's exegetical foundations.

Clearly the recognition that promissory language is performative, with all that this entails, does not in itself provide a context of meaning for everything which Moltmann wishes to say. We must be careful not to claim too much for it. At the least, however, it enables us to account for the importance of "the future" and "the new" without unwarranted recourse to non-linguistic or to extra-linguistic means. In Rule 1, as Searle states it, we have seen that the utterance of a promise logically predicates some future act of the speaker. The "propositional content" of this future which is predicated obviously cannot be logically derived, but that there is a future content predicated is given in the act of promising itself. It is a constitutive fact of promising. To be sure, the content of the new reality of the future finds expression, as far as Christian faith is concerned, in the eschatological hopes of which Scripture is the witness. But these hopes become the hopes of the present day believer insofar as they become present day promises. Since a future act is predicated by a promise, the words of the utterance are not congruent with any present state of affairs *except*—and this is the point of Moltmann's attempted revision of Barth—that of the form of promise itself.

Once this exception is acknowledged and given its proper place in the argument the ambiguity in Moltmann's own theory on the question of the continuity and discontinuity between the promise and the future, and on the question of the *ex nihilo* character of the eschatological *novum*[108] and the fact that "the new is never wholly new" in the sense of unanticipated,[109] is removed. There is one present reality which is not contradicted but confirmed by the future. It is the present reality of the promise of God.[110] If the efficacy of revelation is consistently kept within this word-presence of promise, and not in disregard of the logic of this revelatory form attributed to such conceptions as "the future" and "the new," the claims which Moltmann makes regarding the language of promise and its functions can be meaningfully maintained.

4. *Linguistic evidence for a conception of promise.*

Our fourth, more general, criticism of Moltmann's theory was that, despite its stated aim, it does not uncover the linguistic character of a promise. Now that we have broadened the discussion to take into account what Searle calls the "conditions" and "rules" for promising in ordinary discourse we must determine the extent to which these features may also be said to apply to promissory language in revelation.

If we consider the nine "conditions" for nondefective promising as Searle lists them, clearly the first and the fourth (and to this extent the ninth) present difficulties from a theological point of view. With regard to the others there is nothing in them which is irreconcilable with the exegetical insights concerning biblical eschatology which Moltmann is seeking to develop. One can grant, for example, that in promising as a revelatory language-event the speaker expresses a proposition in the utterance of a sentence, or that in expressing a promise the speaker predicates a future act on his part, or that it is not already obvious to both the speaker and the hearer that the speaker will do the act in the normal course of events, or that the speaker intends to do the action, or that the speaker intends that the utterance of the sentence will place him under an obligation to do the act, or that the speaker intends to produce in the hearer the knowledge that the utterance of the sentence is to count as placing the speaker under an obligation to do the action, that he intends to produce this knowledge by means of the recognition of his intention, and that he intends for his intention to be recognized in virtue of the hearer's knowledge of the meaning of the sentence. Conditions 2, 3, 5, 6, 7, and 8, therefore, do not in principle conflict with the biblical perspective by which Moltmann wishes to be governed.

Condition 1, that normal input and output conditions obtain, on the other hand, would at first glance appear to be more problematic from a theological standpoint. When analyzed, however, it too can be shown to be consonant with Moltmann's claims. The question is whether or not we can say with regard to the promise of God that there are no hindrances to the intelligibility of the speech on the part of either the speaker or the hearer. Clearly we cannot if this condition is taken to mean that faith, i.e., the hearing of the biblical message as promise, is a human possibility or capacity. But this conclusion does not necessarily follow from the stipulation that there must be no hindrances to the intelligibility of the speech on the part of the speaker and the hearer in promising. It is obvious that not everyone who hears the words of a promise, particularly when the linguistic expression is not in the grammatical form of an explicit commissive, hears them *as* a promise. What Condition 1 asserts is that in the speaking and the hearing of a promise, when that situation *does* occur, the words must be intelligible. This intelligibility criterion does not rule out depths of meaning or mystery which any promise, human or divine, may contain. What it recognizes is that a promise cannot properly be said to occur in speech if the factors which constitute speech are not present. Put theologically, to hear one's native tongue may not be to hear the gospel which is being proclaimed in that tongue as God's Word. But to hear the gospel as God's Word is always to hear it in one's native tongue.

Condition 4 presents greater difficulties and cannot as stated be reconciled with any theological characterization of promise which purports to be biblical. It is contrary to Moltmann's claim that one function of the divine promise is to negate or contradict present social reality to say that the hearer would prefer the speaker's doing this act to his not doing it, and the speaker believes that the hearer would prefer his doing the act to his not doing it.[111] Human preference cannot be said to determine God's commitments. Of the nine conditions which

Searle lists it would seem, in any event, that this one is plainly the most dubious. The distinction which is drawn between a promise and a threat, or between a pledge to do something "for you" and a pledge to do something "to you," is itself too arbitrary. However, as Searle expounds the implications of Condition 4 even this stipulation, when rephrased, becomes theologically acceptable. The decisive theological requirement is that the word "need" be substituted for such words as "preference" or "desire." This change Searle allows: "Furthermore, a promise, unlike an invitation, normally requires some sort of occasion or situation that calls for the promise. A crucial feature of such occasions or situations seems to be that the promisee wishes (*needs,* desires, etc.) that something be done, and the promisor is aware of this wish (*need,* desire, etc.)."[112]

With this alteration in Condition 4 (and thus in Condition 9 accordingly) each of the nine conditions which are ascribable to promising as an ordinary speech-act can be said to apply as well to promising as a revelatory language-event. Since this is the case the five "rules" of semantics for determining which indicators of illocutionary force qualify as promissory, therefore, are necessary for an understanding of promise as a theological concept.

This logic of promissory language, it must be underscored, has only dealt with one aspect of Moltmann's theory of revelation. Notwithstanding, this linguistic aspect, as we have seen, is fundamental to the theory. The resources we discover in the work of Austin, Evans, and Searle offer the sort of linguistic evidence required for a coherent accounting of Moltmann's statements regarding the functions of the language of promise. Furthermore, this accounting provides a means for the kind of correlation of theological positions with contemporary modes of self-understanding and world-understanding which Moltmann's own standards mandate. And it does this not with recourse to supernaturalistic explanations, but rather with an appeal to "the common reality."[113]

In exploring the thesis that God is revealed as the language of promise creates the experience of history we have in this chapter focused our attention upon the issue of promissory language. What Moltmann has to say concerning "experience" and "history" will be the subject of discussion in Chapter IV.

CHAPTER IV

THE EXPERIENCE OF HISTORY

Of the claims which Moltmann makes concerning revelation none have evoked as much criticism from American theologians as have those which refer to "experience." Writing in 1970 of the critical responses to his views offered two years earlier at a special symposium held at Duke University while he was a visiting professor there, Moltmann observes, "They emphasized the religious experiences of the present."[1] That this should be the case is not surprising when one takes into account 1) the traditional emphasis in American thought upon the appeal to experience and 2) the statements in Moltmann's theology which appear to reject in principle the validity of such an appeal. The points of dispute on this subject call for further examination. Their implications have not been adequately dealt with on either side.

"The appeal to experience," writes the American philosopher of religion, John E. Smith, "the claim that what we think and say is supported by what we actually find is not a novelty. The appeal is to be found in Aristotle and it appeared in a most powerful and decisive form during the period of the Enlightenment, especially in the writings of the classical British empiricists Locke and Hume. Moreover, the concern for experience and the demand that all thinking be based on what we actually find or encounter has been central to the development of American philosophical thought as represented by Peirce, James and Dewey."[2] To be sure, as Smith is intent to point out, the commitment to empirical method may take a variety of forms. Interpretations of what constitutes experience do differ significantly. Christian theology in America, as Christian theology anywhere, cannot simply be equated with a single philosophical orientation. Yet Smith correctly states the prevailing viewpoint of American theologies and philosophies of religion when he writes, "But it is important to notice that there is no necessary incompatibility between experience and revelation."[3]

When Moltmann's thought first became a subject of American discussion it might have been expected that the question of experience, in its various facets, would immediately emerge at the forefront of the debate. How was one to understand such assertions as "that which is Christian does not correspond to reality that can be known or experienced"; faith can only conceive of God *"contra experientiam"*;[4] Christian statements about hope "do not result from experience"?[5] Most of the participants at the Duke consultation in 1968 were emphatic in their reactions.

Harvey Cox saw in these proposals a reissued Barthianism and expressed his own preference for a theology of hope less kerygmatic, less christological, and more attuned to the sense "that God creates in every man the capacity to hope."[6] Langdon Gilkey countered Moltmann's position with his own insistence that "the presupposition of any meaningful language about God is . . . the continual and immediate presence of the divine in present experience."[7] Van Harvey confessed to finding Moltmann's theory "practically impossible." With regard, for example, to the resurrection appearances, "Moltmann, in short, presupposes just what he denies. He trades on our ordinary (analogous?) reasoning from experience to warrant a judgment about an event to which it is said no analogies apply."[8] Similarly, James Gustafson contended, "For me, and perhaps for many others, a religious basis for hope which is immuned from all possibilities of either support or of negative evidences drawn from experience lacks the credibility that is required for hopefulness to be engendered and to persist."[9] The issue, so it appeared, had been clearly drawn. But had it?

In order to answer this question we must sort out the ways in which Moltmann speaks of "experience" throughout his writings.[10]

REFERENCES TO THE TERM "EXPERIENCE"

There are, in the first place, those passages which appear to reject outright all theological appeals to experience. Examples of these are not difficult to find. We have already taken note of the elaboration of this emphasis in the distinction which Moltmann draws between *Lehrsätze* and *Hoffnungssätze*. "*Lehrsätze* find their truth in their controllable correspondence to available, experienced reality. The hope-sentences of promise, however, must stand in contradiction to presently experienced reality. They do not result from experiences but are the condition for the possibility of new experiences."[11] "The way in which Christian theology speaks of Christ cannot be the way of the Greek *logos* or of descriptive-sentences drawn from experience, but only the way of hope-sentences and promises of the future."[12] In addition, with respect to the biblical grounding of his thought, Moltmann contends that neither Old Testament nor New Testament prophecy "extrapolates" a future out of potentialities which currently exist within the present.[13] From a biblical standpoint one must conclude that "the difference and the creative tension between hope and experienced reality are always the driving forces of ethical and historical activity."[14] Such statements as these are typical of many which have been taken by Moltmann's American critics to mean that any empirical orientation in theology is to be rejected as incompatible with biblical faith.

On the other hand, however, there are numerous references in Moltmann's writings which appear not only to sanction but to mandate theological appeals to experience. One of the conditions, we recall, which is prescribed for the making of Christian theological claims is that whatever is said of God must be correlated with a contemporary understanding of the world and of human identity. "If God is not brought to speech with regard to the self-experience and world-experience of human beings, then theology retreats into a ghetto, and the reality with which human beings have to deal is given up to godlessness."[15] From this second standpoint the biblical grounding of the eschatological position is expressed by saying that "Israel *experienced* the reality of God in its history of exodus, covenant, and promise"[16] and that "Christian eschatology arose from the Easter *experience.*"[17] Similarly, "the power of God who transcends history, is *experienced* by Christians in the midst of history."[18]

We encounter, then, this second set of references which would seem to be irreconcilable with the first. The American criticism of Moltmann's statements regarding experience has largely failed to recognize that Moltmann uses the word "experience" in designating two very different conceptions. Rather than speaking inconsistently of the same thing in two irreconcilable ways, as the juxtaposition of certain selected passages would tend to suggest, Moltmann in fact quite uniformly uses the word "experience" first to explain what the revelatory language of promise is not, and then to explain what it is. Once his own two meanings for this term are understood it becomes clear that the logic of his theory of promissory revelation poses more of a challenge to certain empirically based theologies than has generally been acknowledged—either by Moltmann himself or by his critics.

Assertions such as the following exemplify this dual usage. "There is a difference between future and reality, between hope and *experience*, between exodus and arrival, and it is precisely in this difference that we *experience* history."[19] Or again, this time with regard to cosmological, anthropological, and ontological accounts of the meaning and truth of revelatory language:

> The schemes of verification presented here all presuppose that the validation of what is Christian must consist in the fact that word and reality, word and existence, word and name are congruent, and that truth is experienced in correspondence, conformity, and agreement. The question is whether Christian truth must not burst the immediate correspondences of this concept of truth. . . . If *that which is Christian does not correspond to reality that can be known or experienced,* then the observed contradiction between the word of God and reality can become not only an argument against what is Christian but even an argument against reality. . . . Correspondence to God is only possible through the contradiction; conformity with his word is possible only in confession to the cross; *anticipation of the future of his truth is possible only within the experience of history,* that is, in solidarity with the suffering of the eager expectation of creation.[20]

It is evident in these statements that Moltmann is using the one word "experience" to draw a contrast which is crucial to his argument. Within each of these characteristic passages two seemingly opposite claims appear: 1) "There is a difference between hope and *experience*," or, "That which is Christian does not correspond to known or *experienced* reality"; and 2) "It is precisely in this difference that we *experience* history," or, "Anticipation of the future of his (God's) truth is possible only within the *experience* of history." What may strike us at first glance as a rather obvious self-contradiction is in fact a consistent tendency on the part of Moltmann to use the word "experience" first in a negative and then in a positive way.

The negative sense can be expressed scripturally in the Pauline distinction between hope and sight: "Now hope that is seen is not hope. For who hopes for what he sees?"[21] Hope in this instance is not derived from that which is presently available to sight. If the "seen" is taken to mean the "experiential" then the faith which manifests itself as hope in God's promise cannot be said to rest upon experience. To observe how this biblical notion comes to be explained theologically we need only recall once again Moltmann's appropriation of the argument of Georg Picht's monograph, *Die Erfahrung der Geschichte*. It is Picht, as we have seen, whose differentiation between conceptions of experience has formatively influenced Moltmann's viewpoint. The case for the negative sense in which Moltmann speaks of experience cannot be properly understood apart from Picht's analysis.

Picht begins his analysis by first characterizing the Greek understanding of experience. He focuses his examination on the concept of ἐμπειρία.[22] The distinguishing feature of ἐμπειρία according to Aristotle, is that it has no λόγος. This means that it exhibits no enduring structure of its own which lends itself to knowledge. The λόγος is "the form in which man recognizes what always is";[23] ἐμπειρία, devoid of the λόγος, is limited to the changing and the temporal. The λόγος is necessary for knowledge, as the Greeks defined that term; ἐμπειρία has to do with practice, with those ordinary doings of animals as well as humans, which take place beneath the level of what properly is called knowledge. It is therefore a mistake to think of ἐμπειρία in connection with the derivative term "empiricism" as denoting a theory of perception. The λόγος, not ἐμπειρία, is the ground of all theory and of all science. Since "the boundary between experience and science in Aristotle corresponds to the boundary between what is in time and what is not in time,"[24] we are confronted in Greek thought from the very beginning with a basic distinction between time and eternity, between that which changes and that which always is the same, which becomes translated into a distinction between experience and knowledge.

The examination of ἐμπειρία reveals the extent to which Parmenidean thinking shapes the Greek interpretation of the noncognitive character of experience. In order to demonstrate the way in which this

interpretation has affected Western thought Picht next directs attention
to Kant.

The Kantian theory of experience, which Picht sees as the basis of
"the objective science of modern times,"[25] takes the Greek understanding of *being* and applies it to *experience*. It is the Greek ontological scheme, not the Greek theory of ἐμπειρία, which Kant appropriates. "Objective science . . . has as the sphere of experience the
ontological design of the Greeks."[26] The "I" of Kant's transcendental
apperception, which amidst all phenomenal change gives cognitive
unity to consciousness, is the immutable Absolute of Greek metaphysics
no longer applied to deity but to reason. "Whereas the ἐμπειρία of
Aristotle took up the phenomenon as it shows itself, the empirical
science of modern times reduces the phenomenon to the operational
imposition of objectification. Experience becomes the consciousness
antecedent to a method."[27]

This process of objectification is explained by Picht in the following
manner. In the transition of conceptions from the Greeks to Kant εἶδος
becomes "law"; nature, as φύσις, becomes, in the words of Kant, nature as "the existence of something insofar as it is defined according
to universal laws"; and the universal, καθ' ὅλου, as that catholicity of
being which inheres in the existence of every particular, becomes merely
the universal, κατὰ παντός, which as extrinsic and immutable law
determines the status of all appearances within the understanding.[28]
Thus the Greek ontological scheme is appropriated by modern objective science in terms of law. " 'The legislation of human reason,'
that is Kant's conception of philosophy."[29] By means of this
legitimating objectification experiential data are viewed as discrete,
rather than relational givens. "The presupposition of this objectifying
procedure is the readiness for the fixation of a particular, which the
observer imposes upon the aspect to the exclusion of all other
possibilities which otherwise may still lie within the entity itself."[30]

Returning to Moltmann, we can see that it is precisely this Greek-
Kantian delimitation experience, as Picht has portrayed it, which in-
forms Moltmann's use of the word "experience" in the negative sense.
Neither Greek nor Kantian modes of thought prove adequate for an
eschatological theology. In each case the biblical consciousness of the
divine imminence and the inbreaking of the future upon present reality

are disallowed as factors affecting human knowledge. Hope has no bearing upon perception. Moltmann writes, "If the *eschata* are supra-sensible and as such beyond all possibility of knowledge, then eschatological perspectives are in turn also completely irrelevant for the knowledge of the experienced world."[31] From this standpoint the reason for such claims as, "There is a difference between hope and experience," and, "That which is Christian does not correspond to known or experienced reality," becomes plain and understandable. There is a lack of correspondence, an incongruence, between revelation, as Moltmann conceives it, and experienced reality, as it is conceived in the transition from Parmenides to Kant.

Rather than tailoring the conception of revelation to fit this ad-mittedly widespread philosophic tradition regarding experience, Moltmann argues that it is the conception of experience instead which is in need of a theological reformulation. Within the context of revelation the lack of correspondence between what is promised and what is confirmable by reflection upon the present provides for an otherwise unavailable understanding of experience. In this context incongruence may itself be said to be "experienced" and "known" as the negation of all that forecloses the present to the future. This, in short, is what Moltmann means by his second use of the word, this time a positive reference for biblical faith, "the experience of history." From this standpoint the reason for the second set of claims, that "it is precisely in this difference that we experience history" and that "anticipation of the future of his (God's) truth is possible only within the experience of history" becomes equally plain and understandable.

I think it important to stress that what we discover in Moltmann's twofold references to experience is not reducible simply to a philosophical preference for Heraclitus over Parmenides, or for Hegel, by way of Marx and Bloch, over Kant. At least in principle this is not the situation. On the contrary, the thesis is not that a dynamic or dialectical ontology is to be preferred over a static or transcendental one (though it may well be), but that revelation must itself be allowed to define the boundaries of experience. "In order to come to a real understanding of the eschatological message it is thus necessary to gain an understanding and an openness concerning what is meant by 'promise' in the Old and New Testaments, and how in the broader sense a form of language, thought, and hope which is determined by promise experiences God, truth, history, and human nature.''[32] Experience, as with Barth, is properly to be viewed as the predicate of revelation and not as its subject.

Since this is at least theoretically the position, whatever one's judgments about Moltmann's own adherence to it in practice, the real issue of dispute is not addressed merely by suggesting that what is needed on Moltmann's part is a broader based empiricism, one less dominated by Hume and Kant and more in the tradition of Peirce, James, Dewey, and Whitehead. Obviously Kant's is not the only theory of experience. But that is not the point. What the empirically oriented American theologies have tended to overlook in their reactions to Moltmann is that it is not the rejection of any appeal to experience which separates Moltmann's approach from their own. Rather it is the contention that language, insofar as it serves as a medium of revelation, does not gain its meaning and truth by a referentiality to what already or antecedently is experientially present, no matter how far the boundaries of that putative experience are extended.[33] A promise is not of the same logical type as a symbol which articulates and thereby lifts to the level of conscious referentiality some prelinguistic or formerly unconscious state of being.[34] This is why Moltmann insists that the language of promise does not illumine a prior experience of history which is already in some sense felt or apprehended apart from the instrumentality of this language; it creates this experience. In order to assess this claim properly we must first seek to determine what Moltmann means when he refers to ''history.''

REFERENCES TO THE TERM ''HISTORY''

Because of the variety of ways in which history, like experience, has been conceived since the Enlightenment, it is obvious that no single definition can simply be presupposed. We have given attention to Moltmann's repeated insistence that the revelation of God must be depicted as a matter of history, but until now we have not pressed the question as to what exactly this ''history'' is. The foregoing discussion of experience, in the negative sense in which Moltmann uses this word, has dealt only with what the experience of history is not. Picht's attempt to explain from a Heideggerian standpoint of the historicity of the

Dasein what the experience of history entails is appropriated, as we observed, by Moltmann, with the exception that "promise" is substituted for existential "time" as the key concept. This one substitution, however, demands a logical basis other than the one afforded by Picht's ontological explanation. We must therefore look at Moltmann's own references to the term "history." An examination of these discloses five distinguishable meanings germane to our inquiry which may be briefly set forth as follows.

First, as we have seen and need not elaborate further here, history is initially defined by Moltmann on the grounds of biblical theology as that which occurs between promise and fulfillment. "The promises of God initiate history for Israel and retain the leadership in all historic experiences."[35] In this first instance "history" stands for what is alleged to be a uniquely Hebraic perception of reality.

Second, Moltmann speaks of "history" on a broader scale as a consciousness of mission. Historical consciousness *(Geschichtsbewusstsein)* is mission consciousness *(Sendungsbewusstsein).*[36] This second definition, while in harmony with the first, is presented as having a philosophical as well as a biblical warrant. "From Herder's *Ideen zur Philosophie der Geschichte der Menschheit,* Kant's *Ideen zu einer allegemeinen Geschichte in weltbürgerlicher Absicht,* Schiller's *Was heisst und zu welchem Ende studiert man Universalgeschichte?,* and finally Hegel's *Philosophie der Weltgeschichte,* all historians and historical thinkers have possessed a consciousness of mission and a faith in the meaningfulness of history and the great task of mankind."[37]

Third, Moltmann refers to "history" as a consciousness of social crisis. "The modern consciousness of history is a consciousness of crisis, and all modern philosophy of history is at base philosophy of crisis."[38] With the events of the French Revolution one finds the emergence in Europe of a criticism of thought and institutions which exhibits a new form of consciousness. *Geschichtsbewusstsein* is *Krisenbewusstsein.* Since the time of the French Revolution "history" has been experienced as a "crisis in permanence" or as a "permanent revolution."[39] In this third sense "history" is in its origins a European phenomenon which designates a revolutionary situation in which one finds "a succession of attempts to realize freedom in time by creating a new future in the same place."[40] Moltmann explains: "By 'history' we understand here the experience of reality in conflicts. It is not simply the experience that everything is transitory. Neither is it simply the experience that all things find themselves in the river of time with the present standing between the no–more of the past and the not–yet of the future. Furthermore, it is not only the experience that man must ever and again make decisions. Rather, 'history' is the impression that man together with his society and his world is an experiment and that not only he himself, but also his world, represents a risk.''[41]

Following from this third type of reference, yet to be distinguished from it, is a *fourth* meaning of "history," this time not a form of consciousness, but the room for action opened up in the world itself by revelation. History is "the arena *(Spielraum)* in which the process of adjudicating truth *(Rechtsprozess)* is carried out."[42] The nuance conveyed here by the words *Spielraum* and *Rechtsprozess* is that of a courtroom trial where the final outcome has not yet been established. "History" in this respect is the contested ground of this world's time and space where the lawful rights of the crucified Christ continue to be disputed. The presupposition underlying this third definition is that "history is better grasped in the categories of a legal trial and the conflict over righteousness, life, and freedom than in naturalistic categories."[43]

Finally, Moltmann writes of "history" in the more conventional sense as past recorded events. In this *fifth* instance reference is made not to a practical mode of consciousness or to a particular mode of reality *(Geschichte)*, but to the critical theory or account *(Historie)* given of that consciousness and reality. An eschatological theology, it is contended, cannot as such avoid dealing with historiographical questions.[44] The proper interpretation of past events requires that a theological conception of history based upon an *intellectus fidei resurrectionis* be formulated.[45]

Looking at these five meanings comprehensively, we can say that for Moltmann the term "history" stands for a mode of consciousness, a mode of reality, and the account which is given of their interconnection. Faith as historical consciousness, that is, as consciousness of mission and of social crisis, and reality as history, that is, as the room for action opened up in the world of events itself by revelation, are held to be inseparable. With this conception in mind I want now to turn to

the case which Moltmann presents for claiming that the language of
promise creates the experience of history.

THE RELATION OF THE LANGUAGE OF PROMISE
TO THE EXPERIENCE OF HISTORY

In Moltmann's theory the particular sequence of events to which the
Scriptures bear witness becomes revelatory of God only insofar as it
leads to an ever new recognition of God's faithfulness in the ongoing
process and practice of the apostolic mission. Knowledge of God is thus
to be characterized as a practical, socially involved kind of knowing. It is
properly called historical knowing in the sense that it occurs among
those communities of eschatological expectation where the transformation of this earth's present order is actively sought and celebrated
with reference to worldly events in the light of a hoped for glory already
announced and believed to be impending. History emerges as an issue
precisely because of the perseverance of the saints.[46] "The direction of
the mission is the only constant in history."[47]

What differentiates the Hebraic experience of history as a consciousness of mission from faith as the consciousness of mission today is
the fact that with the rise of historical critical method in the seventeenth
century the equation of tradition with history is no longer implicitly
assumed. Here is the source of the discontinuity between faith as the
experience of history in the biblical context and in the present. "The
critical historical science of the present alienates the past."[48] "The
relationship to history as tradition has become one of reflection and has
lost its immediacy. If we are, therefore, to understand 'history as
tradition' a new conception of tradition must be gained which itself
exceeds historical criticism and its consciousness of the crisis of history
without denying or muzzling it."[49] Systematic theology cannot develop
the present day significance of the biblical tradition of mission, which is
its task, apart from addressing the problem of what constitutes historical significance posed by contemporary philosophies of history.

If we today are to think of "history" in light of the biblical traditions
of *promissio quaerens missionem* four points, Moltmann contends,
must be maintained. 1) Historical knowing is self-involving and world-
transforming, not abstract and world-justifying. 2) In the experience of
history the Cartesian-Kantian epistemological dichotomy between

subjectivity and objectivity and between self-understanding and world-understanding is overcome. 3) Theories of history which seek to foreclose the possibilities of history through projection or prediction and to forestall social change through social control are theologically unacceptable. 4) A theological understanding of history must not resort to precritical forms of thought. Concerning this fourth point Molt-mann writes, "The uncritical use of such terms as 'historical,' 'history,' 'facts,' 'tradition,' 'reason,' etc., in a theological sense serves to indicate that the methodological, practical, and ideological atheism of modern times is being circumvented rather than taken seriously."[50]

This brings us back once again to the explanatory concepts of "tendency" and "latency" which we have previously considered in connection with an examination of the functions of promissory language. Moltmann aims to discover the conceptual means which will make understandable the biblical insight that the promise of God historicizes reality. *What makes an event significant as history?* That is the question which any contemporary theology which seeks to be shaped by the perspective of biblical eschatology must answer. Since the time of Troeltsch especially the complexity of this question of a *Geschichtslogik* has been recognized. Moltmann surveys a variety of attempts to explain historical significance, including the use of such principles as the "law" of cause and effect, the "style" which events exhibit when perceived in their native cultural environment, the "structure" or "form" of the social and institutional context in which historical judgments are reached, and the "self-understanding" of existentialist interpretation.[51] The Blochian concepts are preferred, however, because, as we have quoted Moltmann's own definition earlier, " 'tendency' means something which mediates between the real, objective possibilities and the subjective decisions, and to that extent places the historical 'facts' in the stream of the historical process and the subjective decisions of the historical observer within the same process."[52]

Any model of historical explanation, cautions Moltmann, is to be treated only as a heuristic aid which is logically equivocal because an "unequivocal and eternally established reality is not yet there to be conceived."[53] The notions of "tendency" and "latency" share this limitation. They are not to be given the status of precise metaphysical categories. Nevertheless, since Moltmann appropriates them we may conclude that in his judgment they provide the most adequate contemporary means of explaining the process of history. Their value, if we are to take the words of Moltmann's own description, is apparently to be seen in their capacity to unite objective possibilities with subjective decisions, and historical facts with interpretation, "within the same process." Cause and effect theories of logical positivism and *Heilsgeschichte* theories of revelational positivism are both, in this manner, surpassed. An account can thus be given of history as a mode of consciousness and history as a mode of reality in their interconnection.

The critical test for any theological understanding of what constitutes historical significance is the message of the resurrection of Jesus Christ. Moltmann draws upon the language of "tendency" and "latency" in addressing this problem. He freely acknowledges that "what 'resurrection of the dead' really is and how the raising of Jesus 'actually happened' is something even the New Testament reports of Easter do not claim to know."[54] What occurred between the crucifixion of Jesus and the initiation and perseverance of the mission to the world in his name can only be designated as an eschatological history-making reality for which no presently available historical analogies apply. "The raising of Christ, therefore, is not to be called 'historic' (*geschichtlich*) because it occurred *in* the history which is opened up by some other categories, but rather it is to be called historic because, insofar as it directs the way of future events, it *makes* (*stiftet*) history in which we can and must live."[55] The dynamic of this history-making occurrence of the resurrection is explained by Moltmann as the "tendency" operative in the mission of Christ to make what appears as "latent" in the suffering of the cross into an eschatological process to which all other events of history must finally refer for meaning.

By using the concept of "tendency" Moltmann seeks to maintain two of his major premises without contradiction. On the one hand his opposition to Greek *logos* thinking leads him to insist that the experience of history cannot be explained with reference to anything that is "unchanging, always existing, and equally valid at all times."[56] On the other hand we have seen that promises, though they become transformed in history as far as the reinterpretation of their propositional content is concerned, are said nevertheless to retain their "character" as promises and that, in addition, the direction of mission is described as "the only constant in history." The *character* and *direction* of promise and mission are thus, at least in the logic of Moltmann's case, clearly presented as "unchanging, always existing, and equally valid at all times." Elsewhere he speaks of their orientation toward the future of the crucified Christ as an "invariable" (*Invariante*).[57] By expressing this invariable character and direction of promise and mission as a "tendency" the effort is made to avoid any metaphysical suggestion that history can be understood in terms either of some perdurably static essence or of some organic teleological process. In either case the linguistic form of revelation as a promissory language-event which initiates the experience of history would be denied.

But here we encounter problems with Moltmann's account. As a means of explaining the relation of promise to history the notion of "tendency" proves inadequate in at least three respects. In the first place, and most obviously, it is excessively vague, described only as "something" which mediates between objectivity and subjectivity. Even Moltmann's insistence that the nature of history is such that it cannot be precisely defined, and that it can only be understood in heuristic and logically equivocal models of thought, cannot be taken as a sufficient reason for this conceptual vagueness if the second disciplinary requirement for the making of theological claims, the requirement that prohibits arbitrary assertions, is to be honored. In the second place, there is nothing peculiar to promises about the notion of tendency. The idea is derived from a theory of dialectical world process in which revelatory language in the form of promise is not held to be the initiatory factor. In the case of Bloch the tendency of the not-yet resides within the material process. Revelation does not create it. Various types of anticipatory consciousness in addition to promises—day dreams, wishes, hungers, projections, etc.—can be said to exhibit this tendency. What Moltmann does is transfer Bloch's description of tendency to his own description of revelatory promise. When we read, for example, that revelation in the resurrection is to be understood as a "promise (that) stands between knowing and not knowing, between necessity and possibility, between that which is not yet and that which already is," we are being offered an account that Bloch has originally given of the tendency of the world process.[58] This practice of coalescing two essentially incommensurate concepts, promise and tendency, results in a predisposition on Moltmann's part to speak of the historical significance of the resurrection in some instances as a performative language-event and in others as a dialectical world process without demonstrating how the former is necessary to the latter.[59] "Tendency" says nothing about the intentionality and linguistic conventions which are the constitutive facts of promising. Inevitably the claims which have been made for the language of promise become compromised. The third inadequacy of the use of tendency and latency as principles of explanation is that their status is simply posited and is not accessible to examination. To argue that this status is only heuristic does not exempt Moltmann's position from the charge that, contrary to his stated intention, it is in this respect an arbitrary exercise in revelational positivism. There is no way to adjudicate claims about tendencies and latencies. Thus we must conclude, according to Moltmann's own criteria, that the appropriation of these concepts does not produce a view which qualifies as an "understanding" of the dynamics of revelation.

There yet remains, however, an alternative possibility for explaining the relation of promise to history which is implicit but never developed in Moltmann's discussion of the resurrection. I refer now to several statements which are made concerning the revelatory importance of narrative form. "The New Testament reports of Easter proclaim in the form of narration and narrate history in the form of proclamation. . . . If the reality of the resurrection of Jesus is transmitted and mediated to us only by way of missionary proclamation, and this way of transmission and mediation manifestly belongs to the reality of the resurrection itself, then it must be asked whether the inner necessity of this kind of statement and communication is not grounded in the peculiarity of the event itself."[60] "The gospel, according to its intention, is neither source nor call to decision; rather it narrates proclamation and proclaims narration and thereby speaks of the certainty of existence with regard to factual states of affairs and of factual findings with regard to the illumination of existence. In order to grasp this the reciprocal relationship between existential truth and factual truth must be grasped in a new way."[61]

By opting for Bloch's dialectical thought forms to explain the relation between the existential and the factual, and between the verbal and the real, which may be said to occur in the movement of *promissio quaerens missionem,* Moltmann neglects to pursue the logic of narrative itself. Some further attention to the role of narrative in understanding what constitutes historical significance would appear to be in order.

THE LOGIC OF NARRATIVE

To keep strictly within the scope and single focus of our inquiry certain limits must be imposed at this point. My concern is solely with the question raised by the presence of narrative form in the post-resurrection Christian proclamation, and whether, as Moltmann himself asks, this "kind of statement and communication is not grounded in the peculiarity of the event itself." Is there a clue here to a more coherent way of accounting for the claim that God's Word as promissory language creates history? In addressing this one question I will not undertake to deal with other issues associated with the topic of narrative which are not directly relevant to Moltmann's efforts to bring together in a new way what he calls "existential truth" and "factual truth." Nor should we expect of his theology a full-scale treatment of the relation of language and reality, despite his provocative allusions on the subject. For help in arriving at an answer I shall draw upon a discussion concerning the importance of narrative in historical thinking which first appeared in Anglo-American studies in the philosophy of history in the middle sixties. The subject of narrativist history has called forth an extensive and growing literature. I will confine my remarks primarily to two of the most influential texts on this topic, W.B. Gallie's *Philosophy and the Historical Understanding* and Arthur C. Danto's *Analytical Philosophy of History.*[62] My aim is not to review these texts as such, or to treat them as incontrovertible authorities, but to consider what light they may throw upon the specific theological project we are examining.

I propose now to put three questions to the philosophies of Gallie and Danto. 1. What makes an event significant as history? 2. What part does a sense of the future play in narration? 3. When does a narrative qualify as history, in distinction from merely fiction or myth? The essential conclusions of each of these writers on each of these points can be fairly stated, I think, rather concisely. We will then compare these findings with Moltmann's own position and consider the extent to which they may provide a more intelligible means for consistently maintaining both the claims which are made for the language of promise and the claims which are made for the experience of history.

1. What makes an event significant as history?

Gallie's response to this question forms the thesis of his book. He is concerned, as he tells us in the beginning, with "the concept of a story, regarded as a form of human understanding *sui generis* and as the basis of all historical thought and knowledge."[63] Historical knowing takes, indeed requires, narrative form. The kind of understanding which may be said to emerge from historical knowing differs in this fundamental respect from that of the natural sciences.

After thinking of history in the categories of German Idealism the mere concept of "story" may strike us as superficially simple. At Gallie's hands, however, its analysis uncovers three further conceptions which enable us to recognize at least those factors which are present when in ordinary discourse "historical" meaning is said to occur. These are the factors, detectable in any narration, of "following," "interest," and "conclusion."[64] To become involved in a narrative, or, to speak more broadly, to engage in historical thinking, requires at a minimum that we move forward toward an end. The outcome may not be known, but that there is direction toward an eventual outcome is given with the structure of a story itself. Without this forward thrust and the ability to follow, that is, to find some sequential connection which enables one to continue in this vein, narrative thinking does not happen and, at the most rudimentary level, historical understanding is impossible.

Interest, Gallie contends, can be shown to be equally essential to narration. Not all events of the past become recorded in story, and to this extent not all of the past is given to our historical understanding. Historical significance deals with the human meaning of events. It speaks to human interests. "The lesson to be drawn from these considerations," writes Gallie, "can be expressed in two ways. Negatively, they force us to concede that not all knowledge of the human past is history. Positively, they force us to recognize that there is no history of human beings or societies that cannot and do not, in an extended sense of the phrase, *speak* to us: that do not belong with us in a single—no matter how fragmentary—communication system."[65]

In addition to the factors of following and interest every narration characteristically presupposes a conclusion. We shall look at what Gallie has to say on this point in a moment. It is clear, however, that the idea of an outcome, quite apart from whatever content it may have, is implicit in such acts as constructing, telling, reading, and hearing stories.

Obviously much more is required in order to say why certain stories, unlike others, are accepted as history. But the narrative form, in Gallie's view, is the *conditio sine qua non* for any event to possess historical significance. The purpose of explanations in the discipline of writing history, he argues, is not to do away with, or transcend, this element of story.[66] Rather, explanations are to be thought of as marginal glosses, admittedly of major and not simply trivial consequence, which serve, nevertheless, not to replace a narrative, but "to enable us to follow a narrative when we have got stuck, or to follow again more confidently when we had begun to be confused or bewildered."[67]

Danto's text also provides us with a direct answer to our question: "To ask for the significance of an event, in the historical sense of the term, is to ask a question which can be answered only in the context of a story."[68] "My thesis," Danto writes, "is that narrative sentences are so peculiarly related to our concept of history that analysis of them must indicate what some of the main features of that concept are."[69] A major part of Danto's study is thus given over to a discussion of the logic of "narrative sentences." Such sentences, he argues, comprise a particular class of utterance most apparent in historical writings.

Like Gallie, Danto distinguishes between history and the work of the natural sciences by emphasizing the role of narrative in historical knowledge. Both history and science are said to exhibit a relativism in that neither can pretend to reproduce events or phenomena *in toto* but only to organize their selective data according to certain interests. "We cannot conceive of history," Danto acknowledges, "without organizational schemes, nor of historically organizing schemes apart from specific human interests. . . . The difference between history and science is not that history does and science does not employ organizing schemes which go beyond what is given. Both do. The difference has to do with the *kind* of organizing schemes employed by each. *History* tells stories."[70]

2. What part does a sense of the future play in narration?

In examining the views of both Gallie and Danto the reader is struck by the importance, precisely for historical awareness, which is attached to a sense of the future. Danto criticizes the earlier, pre-analytical (he labels them "substantive") philosophies of history which seek to be universal in scope as "essentially theological." Their fallacy is that they exhibit a "prophetic" manner of speaking about the future—that is, they speak "of the present in the light of a future treated as a *fait accompli*"—whether they be confessedly theistic or secular.[71] The analytical philosophers of history, however, as we can see from these texts of Gallie and Danto, while they do not argue from the same universalist and providential assumptions, and are not "theological" in that sense, nevertheless, continue to stress in their own way the crucial factor of the future.

Developing his examination of "following," "interest," and "conclusion," Gallie writes, "Following a story . . . is a teleologically guided form of attention. We are pulled along by our sympathies towards a promised yet always open conclusion, across any number of contingent, surprising events, but always on the understanding that they will not divert us hopelessly from the vaguely promised end."[72] A sense of the future, however hidden and unspecified, may thus be said to be disclosed in the logical structure of narration insofar as a conclusion is presupposed. In this regard, if in no other, one may recognize an influence of the future over the present without which historical experience does not occur. "Without being predicted, and often without being even vaguely foreseen, the conclusion of a story nevertheless guides our interest almost from the start."[73]

It is further worthy of remark that Gallie clearly differentiates historical knowing from knowledge as a means of control. Following a story, he explains, is "not to command or forestall events, but to find them intellectually acceptable after all—i.e., after all the shock and the surprise that their coming may well at first have caused us."[74] Gallie would thus avoid any inference of historical predictability in his references to "conclusion" as a sense of the future implicit in the form of narrative itself.

On this question Danto, for his part, takes a rather different tack. Of narrative sentences he writes, "Their most general characteristic is that they refer to at least two time-separated events though they only *describe* (are only about) the earliest event to which they refer."[75] Historical comprehension, as a description of events, is thus possible only from the standpoint of a future looking back. "The whole truth concerning an event can only be known after, and sometimes only *long* after the event itself has taken place, and this part of the story historians alone can tell. It is something even the best sort of witness cannot know."[76] "For the whole point of history is *not* to know about actions as witnesses might, but as historians do, in connection with later events and as parts of temporal wholes."[77] The awareness of what historical significance involves, as a looking back, is thus dependent upon an awareness of the future, a looking forward. And what we are aware of vis-à-vis the future is that we cannot claim to know it as we do the past. "It is illegitimate to make, about the future, the kinds of statements it is legitimate to make about the past."[78] What we do know is that our knowledge of the past is limited by our lack of knowledge of the future. Thus Danto writes, "Completely to describe an event is to locate it in all the right stories, and this we cannot do. We cannot because we are temporally provincial with regard to the future."[79] "Speculative philosophers of history, indeed, have at times regarded the whole of history as exhibiting some divine plan which they regard as their duty to discern, or which they credit themselves with having already discerned in part, perhaps through revelation."[80] These views, however, Danto argues, all rest upon the false assumption of some "precognition" of future events which is of the same evidential status as memory.[81]

Summing up these two discussions, one can say that whereas Gallie sees a forward thrust toward the future in the notion of conclusion implicit within the logic of narration itself, Danto is intent to emphasize instead the temporal position of the narrator as necessarily future to all events which permit of his narration. Where each is alike is in his contention that the logic of narration, and thus of historical understanding, exhibits a sense of the future.[82]

3. When does a narrative qualify as history, in distinction from merely fiction or myth?

The reply which Gallie offers to this third question is based upon an earlier discussion by Collingwood which, in turn, appeals to Ranke's celebrated axiom that history seeks to record "what actually happened" (*wie es eigentlich gewesen*).[83] Though both the novelist and the historian are involved in the task of providing what Collingwood calls a "coherent picture," and Gallie, a "followable narrative," the historian, Collingwood and Gallie agree, must be bound by three requirements which are not demanded of the novelist.[84]

> 1. The historian's picture must be located in space and time.
> 2. "All history must be consistent with itself. Purely imaginary worlds cannot clash and need not agree; each is a world to itself. But there is only one historical world, and everything in it must stand in some relation to everything else . . ."
> 3. The historian's picture "stands in a peculiar relation to something called evidence."

With regard to Collingwood's second condition, that "there is only one historical world," Gallie offers this further clarification.

> The one historical world, I should like to suggest, is an intellectual ideal or device which is essential for the practice of history as we know it; but its location, if it must be given one, is in the heads, because in the hopes of historians. To speak more exactly: the one historical world is an idea without any definite descriptive content, indeed it is not an empirical idea at all. It is comparable, rather, with a Kantian ideal of reason (as regulatively employed) . . .[85]

Thus the requirement that all history be of a piece and consistent with itself, in Gallie's view, has its source in "the hopes of historians." It is "a demand laid upon the conscience, a challenge set to the passion, of any and every historian."[86] The "one historical world" is not a "quasi-substantial" reality existing independently of human interests. Ranke's principle is allowable only if the interest factor is taken into account. "But history is not just past human actions. . . . It is our name for the study of any past human action insofar as it is understood through its interconnectedness with other actions which a particular community or generation regards as of special interest to *them*."[87]

In addition to Collingwood's three criteria for distinguishing historical narratives from those of fiction or myth Gallie proposes a fourth of his own. "The received materials out of which they are formed and the final use to which they are submitted give them an emphatically public character."[88] The historian cannot appeal to evidence which in principle is not open to others. When these four criteria are applied the final test of a historical understanding becomes a matter of asking if we have arrived at "the best narrative that we can get" in the sense of one that is "consistent, plausible, and in accordance with all the evidence."[89]

Danto's discussion does not differ essentially from Gallie's at this point. The aim of the historians is "to try to make true statements, or to give true descriptions, of events in their past."[90] In attempting to narrate the past truthfully with concern for *wie es eigentlich gewesen* one cannot pretend to divorce fact from interpretation, and interpretation from interest, and thus present in some bare chronicle "an imitation or duplication of the past."[91] We can, nevertheless, distinguish historical narrative from that of fiction or myth in that history must be supported by "*documentary* evidence." To be sure, what constitutes evidence in historical narration is not of a single logical type, and, as Danto points out, even the fact that we employ general concepts to label individuals—doctor, lawyer, merchant, chief—means that the plausibility of our stories is supported not only by documents and records but, in part, by "*conceptual* evidence" as well. But the basic point remains that a narrative qualifies as history only if there is publicly accessible documentation sufficient to back up its plausibility. This requirement explains why, for example, a narrative of future events is unacceptable as history. Of the future, Danto writes, "we have *only* conceptual evidence, and no documentary evidence at all . . . and, for this reason, our conception of the future has a curiously open and curiously abstract quality about it."[92]

Having noted the views of Gallie and Danto with respect to our three questions concerning the role of narration in historical understanding, let us now look once again at Moltmann's claims regarding promissory language and the experience of history.

From the standpoint of Moltmann's own position, despite the different philosophical mold in which it is cast, it would appear for several reasons that we are warranted in introducing these insights of the analytical philosophers of history into our considerations. They speak directly to the issue of narrative form, to which Moltmann makes reference in his discussion of the resurrection proclamation. They represent a major contemporary mode of thinking of the sort with which, Moltmann advises, theology must seek to be in working association. And they are obviously relevant to the task that Moltmann sets of spelling out the implications of an eschatological theology at the level of contemporary historiographical debate.

The dissimilarities between Moltmann's approach and that of Gallie and Danto are, of course, evident to any reader who moves from the one context of thought to the other and are to be acknowledged as well. The analytical philosophies are primarily concerned with history as a record of the past. They treat the problems associated with historical understanding from the viewpoint of a historian's writing and research. Their language does not come from the tradition of German Idealism, with its stress upon a dialectical reading of events, and we do not find their discussions couched in such terms as "historical consciousness" and "reality as history." Furthermore, I am not suggesting that we think of the theories of Gallie and Danto, and even of the narrativist position in general, as themselves incontestable or conclusive.[93] Where Moltmann and these writers do join the issue in a mutually illuminating fashion, however, is on the role of narration in determining historical significance, and it is at this one basic point that I wish to bring their views into comparison.

Clearly we cannot say within the analytical context of Gallie and Danto that the resurrection of Jesus Christ is a historical event. The requisite, publicly accessible documentation to support such a statement obviously is not available. But Moltmann's position is in complete agreement here. It is a misunderstanding of the eschatological newness of the resurrection, he argues, to say that it conforms to any presently existing, or potentially ascertainable, criteria of what qualifies as historical event. The resurrection, as the "setting-in-force" of God's promise, cannot properly be said to have taken place *in* history; rather it *makes* history. In the language of the narrativists to *make* history is to *generate* a story. Moltmann's claim, translated into these terms, would read: the resurrection does not conform to the generally accepted criteria for determining historical events; rather, it is narrative-generating in such a way that it gives historical significance to events, such as the life and death of Jesus and the mission of his followers, for which there is documentary evidence. That a narrative was generated can be seen in the gospel proclamation of Easter, and that it continues to be generated can be seen in the ongoing mission and proclamation of this gospel.

Still our problem is not so easily solved. For under the conditions articulated by Gallie and Danto, and essentially subscribed to by all historians today, the story constituted by the resurrection does not itself qualify as a historical narrative. Insofar as it includes references to the Risen Christ this narrative must be regarded as either fiction or myth. To judge these references by Gallie's four points: they present a picture not located only in space and time; they are not consistent with what we know of other events in our one historical world; they do not stand in the necessary relation to something called evidence; and the materials out of which they are formed and the use to which they are submitted do not give them the requisite "public" character.

What can be argued, I propose, is that this narrative, precisely because of its non-historical references to a Risen Christ, functions to make events which *do* conform to the conditions for historicality—the events of the fact and death of Jesus and the beginning and perseverance of the witnessing mission—historically significant in a manner which otherwise would *not* allow, in Gallie's words, "the best narrative that we can get" in the sense of one that is "consistent, plausible, and in accordance with all the evidence." If the point can be granted that not all narratives which properly may be said to provide historical significance contain *only* historical references, then it is difficult to see how in principle there can be any necessary reason in the logic of narrative for denying that the story generated by the resurrection may properly be said to create history.[94]

Both Gallie and Danto acknowledge the presence of selective "interests" and "organizing schemes" in historical understanding. And, more importantly, both, in differing ways, recognize that a reference to the future is constitutive of a historical reference to the past. What Gallie and Danto each deny is that this reference to the future is of the same logical type as a reference to the past. But this is exactly the point of Moltmann's distinction between "descriptive sentences" and "hope sentences." For Moltmann also, references to the resurrection are nondescriptive and logically unlike descriptive references to the past. What Moltmann, for his part, fails to make clear in this connection is that *Hoffnungssätze* appear in Christian proclamation only in conjunction with *Lehrsätze*. The references to the future cannot be abstracted from descriptive references to the past.[95] This the narrativists help us to see. It is a point reenforced by the findings of Austin, Evans, and Searle in their investigations of promissory language. The illocutionary force of a promise as a commissive is distinguishable but not separable from its propositional content. Applied theologically these insights help to explain why an understanding of revelatory language requires that the two concepts of promise and narrative be interpreted together. In the witnessing message as received in faith a narrative functions as a promise and a promise is heard in the form of a narrative. Revelatory language is promissory narration.

What the theories of Gallie and Danto, for their part, do not take into account is the possibility of a narrative reference to the future which, while clearly not of the same logical type as a descriptive reference to the past, is nevertheless different also from either the teleological thrust of a narrative toward its conclusion, which Gallie emphasizes, or the awareness of the unknowability of the future as a limit upon our capacity to tell the story of the past and present, which Danto stresses. There is, as we discussed in Chapter III, a reference to the future, or, more exactly, a relation to the future predicated by the self-involving logic of a promise. Whenever narratives function to convey promissory meaning this sort of future relation must be given its due. It is not to be mistaken for a claim to historical foreknowledge. Danto commits this error when he oversimplifies the theological options with regard to history by characterizing them merely as abortive efforts to treat the future "prophetically" as a *"fait accompli"* in the name of a historical foreknowledge gained via revelation. Such a generalization, while apt in some cases, plainly does not apply to the logic of Moltmann's theology of revelation. Quite the opposite of a presumption to know the concluded story of the future as a narrative of historical events is Moltmann's interpretation of the prophetic eschatological sense as, to borrow Gabriel Marcel's telling phrase, a "memory of the future," which in recalling the past looks on it as a pledge of God's faithfulness in the uncertainty of current and coming events. Here the correlate of memory is not "precognition," as Danto alleges, but "promise." This puts the relation to the future not on the level of speculative clair-voyance, but on the level, to recall the language offered by Evans, of self-involvement as a correlative performative. Trust in the promise of God's faithfulness and coming vindication in all things is a factor which continues to generate the narrative means necessary for historical significance. From this self-involving relation of promissory narration to the future it follows that the "hope" for "one historical world," as Gallie puts it, is not simply an intellectual demand of reason for unified comprehension. It is a "passion"—also his word—for a universal righteousness and freedom promised in the resurrection message. This self-involving, and thus world-transforming, character of historical experience Moltmann's theory of revelation will not allow us to overlook.[96]

Finally, to return to the question of "experience" with which this chapter began, the understanding of historical significance in terms of a logic of promise and of a logic of narrative enables us to see why it may be said that eschatological faith as "the experience of history" does not have its basis in present experience. If revelatory language occurs as promissory narration, it cannot be held that it gains its meaning and truth by referring to some already existing human awareness. Narration is a prerequisite for historical experience, and the promissory function of the resurrection references which are the focal point of the gospel proclamation keep this narrative from being a timeless figuration of present states of affairs. Neither promises nor narratives are thus reducible to the logical order of symbolic utterance in which ordinary means are said to represent at once some allegedly higher meaning.[97] Revelation in the mode of promissory narration does indeed bear a relation to present experience, as Moltmann reiterates. But by granting historical significance to worldly events encountered in the world-transforming mission of the Risen Christ, and by creating the hope for "one historical world" of righteousness and freedom, this relation is not properly depicted as one of symbolic reference to things as they presently are.[98] The present is not disregarded, but neither is it merely illumined. It is, as Moltmann contends, critically called into question.

The logic of the narrativist position with regard to history, when supplemented by the logic of promissory language, offers alternative resources for accounting for the meaning and truth of this theological claim. Such an accounting, in any comprehensive sense, would extend beyond the bounds of our subject.[99] But enough has been said, I believe, to suggest the conceptual possibilities which are available.

We come now to the third of the three central sets of issues which Moltmann's theory of revelation presents. What is Christian theology enabled to say of the being of God and of the reality of the world from the eschatological standpoint, as Moltmann has drawn it, of the language of promise and the experience of history? What ontological judgments does this view of divine revelation permit?

CHAPTER V

THE QUESTION OF AN ESCHATOLOGICAL ONTOLOGY

"The furthermost horizon of eschatology," Moltmann writes, is "the eschatology of being. Hope in the coming God leads not only to a messianic interpretation of biblical and of Christian history but must, if it is to be relevant, lead also to a messianic understanding of reality itself."[1] This call for a theological development of an eschatological ontology can be found throughout Moltmann's writings. "The first task of eschatological theology in debate with transcendence theology and immanence theology is to define more closely the mode of God's being."[2] "Without eschatological ontology, eschatological existence is inexpressible."[3] If revelation is indeed the promise of a "new creative act" in the coming of God's kingdom, then this means that we "must develop an eschatology of all things."[4] The ontological question for Moltmann is clearly not extraneous to or in contradiction with a biblical understanding of revelation; rather, it is implicit within it.[5]

We should not expect to find in Moltmann's initial proposals concerning promissory revelation a comprehensive outline of an eschatological ontology. Nor should we overlook the subsequent development of his thought as it has moved from revelation to the doctrine of the crucified God and to such other traditional loci of Christian theology as the church, the Holy Spirit, human existence, and creation. The scope of this essay, however, includes only the ontological consequences of the specific claims which Moltman has made for revelation in the language and history of promise. Our topic is promissory revelation—as posed by Moltmann—and not whether Moltmann presently holds to his original position on this subject.

According to his own judgment, his later writings to date complement his initial view but do not retract it. In *The Crucified God* we are advised that the "theology of the cross" is to be read as "none other than the reverse side of the Christian theology of hope."[6] In *The Church in the Power of the Spirit* Moltmann again writes: "We take the eschatological point of departure in understanding the history of Christ by asking the meaning of that history. The promise, the use, and the aim are all included in the modern word 'meaning.' What we have called 'the interest of Christ' and the 'tendency' of his history are also inherent in it."[7] Essentially the same claims regarding promise are before us. Only now the argument seeks to link resurrection and crucifixion, the Spirit and the church, eschatology and history—indeed, promise and narrative—even more firmly together: "The past can be narrated, and every narration, like enumeration, starts at the beginning and then comes to the end. But along the line of eschatological anticipation the last must be first, the future goes before the past, the end opens up the beginning, and objective time-relationships are reversed. 'History as memory' and 'history as hope,' in that 'hope in the mode of memory' which defines Christian faith, cannot contradict each other, but rather must complete each other."[8] What, then, are the ontological implications of this position?

REVELATION AND BEING: THE ISSUES

At the end of Chapter II we noted that one cannot speak of God's presence "in the form of promise," of the "apocalypse of the promised future," and of God's selfhood (and even tri-unity) as "historical faithfulness" without at least by inference proposing certain ontological delineations. We must now attempt to locate more exactly what problems arise in Moltmann's theory of revelation in the making of these proposals.

First, there are the questions which have to do with an understanding of God's own being. If God is revealed in the language and history of promise, are we to say that the very mode of God's being, that the divine selfhood, is in some sense promissory? To this question, in the logic of Moltmann's case, the answer is clearly, yes. The issue then becomes, in what sense?

In Moltmann's writings four main ontological descriptions of the divine being are advanced. These include the designation of God's reality 1) as Future, 2) as Person, 3) as Crucified, and 4) as Triune. Our task will be to see how the ontological description fits the theory of promissory revelation in each of these cases.

In addition to the questions pertaining to an interpretation of God's being there are, in the second place, the related issues which have to do with the world and with human being. Since the knowledge of God is to be correlated with world-understanding and self-understanding, an eschatological theology requires that attention be given to an eschatological cosmology and anthropology. We cannot attempt to do more in this second instance than consider the most general description which Moltmann's theory presents, that of reality as a historical process. How is the claim that revelation, as "apocalypse," opens up the world to the future of God's truth to be conceived? In the perspective of biblical apocalyptic, Moltmann explains, we discover "the beginning of an eschatological cosmology or an eschatological ontology for which being becomes historic and the cosmos opens itself to the apocalyptic process."[9] Elsewhere we read that this eschatological ontology, if consistent with revelation, cannot be one which is "identical with a metaphysics of entelechy or finality" or with a "philosophy of history pertaining to integral purpose series."[10] Teleological views of world process are to be ruled out. Imminence rather than organic emergence is to be stressed as the root metaphor of such an ontology. Most especially, "coming" is not to be confused with "becoming." These are the proposals which now invite our attention.

THE GOD OF PROMISE

Let us look first at each of the four main ontological descriptions which Moltmann offers of the being of God.

1. God as Future

The first designation is that of "the future as mode of God's being."[11] What does it mean to say that, rather than conceiving of ultimate reality in the categories either of transcendence or of immanence, we are to think of eschatological imminence? Most basically, in Moltmann's view, it is to acknowledge that as the imminent One, God is at once both transcendent and immanent being in the only sense in which these terms can properly be eschatologically understood. To quote the words of Ernst Bloch once again, "The forward-look has replaced the upward-look."[12] "God is not 'beyond us,' but ahead of us in the horizons of the future opened to us in his promises. Thus the 'future' must be considered as mode of God's being."[13] The term "future" with respect to God does not apply, as we might at first suppose, merely to our temporal way of knowing. Rather it is to be taken as an ontological and not simply an epistemological or noetic category. We must think "of the temporal category of the future as belonging to the reality of God."[14] For this reason Moltmann can write, "Therefore, the future as mode of God's being also contains that which formerly was called his eternity."[15] "God," he asserts, "is the power of the future. God is the power of the new."[16] To ascribe ultimate reality to the future is not to think of it either as "fate," or as "caprice," but rather as the "ontological possibility" of newness and the "anthropological freedom" which this affords.[17]

The influence of Bloch is apparent in these ontic descriptions. Where Moltmann distinguishes his own position from that of Bloch is not in the use of the word "future" but in its definition. Instead of conceiving of the future as *futurum*, eschatological theology must seek to develop the significance of *adventus*. This distinction between the future as *futurum* and the future as *adventus* is thus essential to the ontological conception of God as Future. Moltmann writes, "The *futurum* is future participle of *fuo*, and corresponds to the Greek *phyo*, with the noun *physis*. . . . *Physis* is the producing, the eternally begetting womb of all things. *Physis* is divine. What will be emerges from the eternal process of the becoming and begetting of being. It is actualization of the primordial potential."[18] "*Zukunft* (future), by contrast, is a literal translation of *adventus* and *parousia*, wherein the tone of the advent expectation in the messianic spirit of the prophets and apostles has been articulated."[19] Therefore, the *adventus Dei* is not to be confused with the *futurum* of being. "God's being does not lie in the process of the world's becoming. . . . God's being is coming. He is not a 'God with futurum as mode of being' (Bloch), but with the *Zukunft* (future) as his mode to act upon the present and the past."[20] In contrast to a metaphysics of emergent organic process Moltmann in this instance would have us be guided by the idea of *adventus* rather than *futurum*, of coming rather than becoming, of *parousia* rather than *ousia*, of imminence rather than immanence.[21] The intention is to make the description of God as Future consistent with what has been said of revelation in the form of promise.

The extent to which this consistency is achieved depends upon three factors. With regard to revelatory language, as we have seen in Chapter III, the problem is to show how *adventus* is connected with promising. If *adventus* is given an ontological reality apart from promissory language, it has, despite Moltmann's efforts to distinguish it, simply taken over the role of Bloch's *futurum*. With regard to revelatory history, as we have seen in Chapter IV, the problem is to show how *adventus* is connected with ordinary time, with *chronos*. Unless such a connection can be demonstrated this sense of God's eschatological coming hangs, as it were, in thin air and is fundamentally no different from either the so-called transcendentalist or existentialist views of revelation, with their talk of "eternal moment" and *"kairos,"* against which Moltmann protests. And in the third place, with regard to the ontological notion of "future" itself, if we are to ascribe this category to God's own being and to think of "coming" and "imminent arrival" as characterizations of deity "containing" eternity, are we not logically back with Parmenides—eternal *parousia*, if not eternal *ousia?* If, on the other hand, the eternal being of God is held to be other than the temporal categories of promising, imminence, and coming we are faced with two alternatives. Either we must conclude that there is no revelation of God's own being, or, what in effect amounts to the same thing, we must say that God's being essentially changes in the final consummation. To this second option we shall return in a moment.

The alternative ways of accounting for the meaning of Moltmann's claims which we have considered lead to a more restrained and cautious manner of speaking of God as Future. At the same time they do suggest the guidelines for what I take to be a more intelligible and consistent postion, and therefore a more creditable case. From our analysis of the language of promise in Chapter III we may appeal to the recognition that the utterance of a promise logically predicates some future act on the part of the speaker. The predication of this future can be shown to be a constitutive fact of promising. A connection between the future of the revealer and the act of promising can thus be said to be given in the event of revelation. From our analysis of the experience of history in Chapter IV we may appeal to the recognition that promissory revelation may be understood to create history through the medium of narration. Thus *adventus* may be said to connect with *chronos* as promise to narrative, not simply as a conclusion to a sequence of historical happenings, but as the relation to the future which generates the narrative means necessary for historical significance. Without the sense of the future of God given in the promissory character of the resurrection proclamation, it can be argued, the story most in accord with the documentary evidence of what took place *sub Pontio Pilato* and what continues to take place in the witnessing mission could not be told. As far as a logical return to Parmenides is concerned, these alternative types of explanation enable us to see that, if one should wish to speak of an eternal future, this is not the same as speaking of an "epiphany of eternal presence." The difference is that in the case of the former a narrative continues to be generated; the story goes on. Because the role of language essential to both promise and narrative can be uncovered, an account given in these terms is, according to Moltmann's own conditions, neither arbitrary nor equatable with ontological descriptions such as those teleologies of organic emergence which he rejects under the label of the Greek view of *physis*.

2. God as Person

In proposing a conception of deity as constancy of commitment, or as historical faithfulness (*Selbigkeit*), rather than as transcendental selfhood (*Ichheit*), Moltmann registers his objection, as we have seen, to what he considers to be an exaggerated personalism in much of modern theology. Referring to Zimmerli's portrayal of revelation according to the Old Testament as "self-presentation," characterized by the formula, "And they shall know that I am Yahweh," Moltmann observes that "the personalistic descriptions of the self-revelation of God seem to stand in a certain tension with the recognized theological significance of the promise." He writes, "If the revelation of God is to be understood in such a personal way, why *must* the self-presentation of Yahweh find its explication in the word of promise? But if promise is constitutive for the revealing of Yahweh, then does not more lie in the formula of self-presentation than merely a self-disclosing of the mystery of a person—

namely a pledge of faithfulness which points to coming events.''[22] The historical character of revelation is forfeited when theology speaks of the knowledge of God simply in terms of I-Thou encounters. The pledge of faithfulness which points to coming events and which is known only in conjunction with events must also be taken into account.

Much of Moltmann's description of God's being is phrased in the language of "process." God is to be understood ontologically as an eschatological process that sets in motion a historical process. On the face of it this language might appear to allow for an impersonal, almost mechanistic, view of deity. "What do we mean by the word 'God'?" Moltmann asks. "He is the power of world transformation in vicarious suffering. . . . He is the word of the justification of the godless. . . . He is the strength of freedom in self-surrender. . . . He is the power of a qualitatively new future. Finally, who is 'God' in the new creation? He is the eternal presence of the victory of the crucified Christ.''[23] The language of "power," "word," "strength," and "presence of victory" applied to God's being would not appear to necessitate person-talk. Such terminology in itself fails to indicate why the question of God's reality in biblical faith is a ''who'' question in which the personal pronoun is appropriate.

In *The Crucified God* Moltmann again returns to this problem.

> ''What sense does it make to speak of 'God'? I think that the unity of the tension-filled and dialectical history of Father and Son and Spirit in the cross on Golgotha allows itself to be described—subsequently, so to speak—as 'God'. . . . Whoever speaks in Christian terms of God must narrate the history of Jesus as a history between the Son and the Father. 'God' then does not mean another nature, or a heavenly person, or a moral court of appeal, but in fact a 'happening' (*Geschehen*). . . . Is there then no 'personal God'? If 'God' means a happening can one pray to him? To a happening one does not pray. Indeed there is no 'personal God' as a person projected in heaven.''[24]

Moltmann's explanation at this point is to say that we can speak, nevertheless, in trinitarian terms of "persons in God" and depict the act of prayer as praying *in* this happening rather than *to* this happening. "The Trinity is no self-contained circle in heaven, but rather an open eschatological process on earth for human beings which proceeds from the cross of Christ.''[25]

Here the promissory character and the narrative character of revelation prove indispensable, I think, to a coherent description. Personal reality is disclosed precisely in the making and keeping of promises, in acts of commitment and covenant. Equally is the term "person" applicable only to one of whom a story of commitments and constancy can be told.[26] To appeal to the classical Trinitarian usage of the Greek *prosopon,* or the Latin *persona,* is not sufficient in itself to justify the claim that God is personal being. An eschatological and historical "process" may be said to reveal a personal reality only if that process is understood to be instituted and constituted by the giving and keeping of promises.[27] Conceived in this manner it is not required that one differentiate, as Moltmann does, between revelation of God in Jesus Christ *ad personam* and *ad opera* and assert that the former is "concluded" (*abgeschlossen*) while the latter remains "yet to be completed" (*unabgeschlossen*).[28] "Person," understood from the standpoint of promissory narration, includes a relation to a still-outstanding and future act. This fact makes it somewhat problematic to distinguish God's "person" from God's "essence" and to argue that the "person" of God as Alpha and Omega is one and the same, but that in respect to the divine "essence" Omega is more than Alpha.[29] Instead one may say that the personal identity of God as Promisor is "one and the same" but that the keeping of a promise adds something new to the making of it. This "more" cannot, however, be said to be of an "essence" other than that of the "person" without denying that God's essence is promissory as revealed.

It would be foolish even to appear to suggest that all ontological problems associated with the conception of God as a personal deity are resolvable purely by thinking of revelation as promissory narration. What I do suggest is that talk of God as Person within such a framework of intelligibility can be shown to be something other than simply poetic license.

3. God as Crucified

From the start Moltmann has been concerned to interpret Christian eschatology as an *eschatologia crucis.*[30] It is in the event of suffering and death on the cross under Pontius Pilate that we may speak of the "incarnation" of God in human flesh. The question for Christian theology thus becomes, "But how can the death of Jesus on the cross be understood as God's act, even as God's suffering?"[31] Without this anchor in the events which took place publicly *sub Pontio Pilato* Christian faith loses its historical character.

We must ask then how adequately Moltmann's efforts to answer the question of the suffering of God maintain this historical anchorage. His argument may be condensed as follows. In the crucifixion of Jesus of Nazareth Christian faith beholds not only the self-identification of God but also, and through this, something which can only be described, however awkwardly, as God's self-differentiation. "The cross of Jesus, understood as the cross of the Son of God, therefore reveals a confrontation (*Umkehr*) within God, an inner-godly *stasis:* 'God is other.' And this happening within God is the happening on the cross."[32] Ultimate reality, apprehended from this perspective, is not conceivable in the categories of classical monotheistic metaphysics. Rather than thinking of the Ultimate and the Absolute as being beyond pathos and passion, because beyond materiality and physical change, we are to define the word "God" in the light of the cry of Jesus, "My God, my God, why hast Thou forsaken me?" But if this is indeed taken to be the paradigmatic event in which God is revealed, and if indeed here we behold God calling out to God, then ultimate reality must further be said to be not only self-identifying and self-differentiating but even self-forsaking. God, and not only the human Jesus, must be portrayed ontologically as crucified.

The modern notion of "the death of God," as Moltmann observes, derives from Hegel at the beginning of the nineteenth century. The dialectic in which the resurrection "over reaches" the crucifixion becomes in Hegel the dialectical process pervading all reality.[33] In the *Theology of Hope* Moltmann adds this corrective: "Only, the god-forsakenness of the cross cannot, as according to Hegel, be made into an impulse of an immanent divine process. A theology of the dialectical self-movement of absolute Spirit would then be only a modification of the dialectical epiphany of the eternal as subject. Hegel sought to reconcile faith and knowledge but at the price of annulling the historicity of the revelation event and understanding it as an eternal event. 'For concept cancels time.' "[34] Without the story of the cross in its relation to the historical Pilate, to *chronos,* there would be no historical expression of God's promise. In *The Crucified God* less explicit attention is given to the category of promise, and Hegelian thought forms are more in evidence. The idealist ingredients of the ontic descriptions are less under control. "Jesus' death cannot be understood 'as the death of God' but only rather as death *in* God."[35] "If one describes the inner trinitarian life of God as 'the history of God' (Hegel), then this history of God contains within itself the entire abyss of god-forsakenness, of absolute death, and of the not-God."[36] Moltmann seeks to avoid the charge that he himself has annulled the historicity of the revelation event in resorting more and more to Hegelian concepts by insisting that "the history of Christ is the inner life of God himself."[37]

But what can the expression "the history of Christ" mean if we keep in mind what has been said about revelation? It cannot with consistency mean less than the narrated significance of the Jesus who was crucified outside the gates of Jerusalem in the first century. Nor can it mean more, if by more is meant something other than this. If it is said to mean less, then the narrative materials essential to historical significance, in any generally accepted sense, are lost. If it is said to mean more, then it is hard to see what is to prevent the historicity of the event, in all but name only, from being relinquished in favor of an Idealistic metaphysics. Saying this does not limit "the history of Christ" in the world to the first century Jesus if one takes into consideration, as one must, the continuance of this narration from the standpoint of ever new situations in the ongoing mission of the Christian movement. Thus do events gain their significance as history. But it does firmly anchor that history in the time and space and struggle of human affairs. Christian faith may convincingly speak of ultimate reality as cruciform only insofar as it attests (and this of course by its life and not merely by its logic) that the story of the sufferings of the present time cannot be told apart from the story of One crucified under Pontius Pilate in whom there is the promise to all sufferers of a glory that is yet to be revealed.

As Moltmann rightly sees, the ontological descriptions of God as Future, and as Person, and as Crucified require that further thought be given to a doctrine of the Trinity. To speak of a self-differentiation and a self-forsaking within God's "inner life" in the historical crucifixion of

Christ leads us to ask what sense such conceptions make in view of the traditional Christian affirmation that God is triune.

4. God as Triune

Moltmann's initial objection to Barth's view of the Trinity is that it interprets the person and history of Jesus Christ as a "fixed and presupposed" reality.[38] In *The Crucified God* the criticism is again made of Barth that, despite the prominence which is given to the Trinity in the structure of the *Church Dogmatics,* the being of God is nevertheless still, in the final analysis, conceived as a simple unitary aseity in terms which do not take the radical consequences of a trinitarian notion of ultimate reality, christologically formulated, seriously. The distinction between the "primary objectivity" of God— God *a se* in the eternal triunity of the divine life—and the "secondary objectivity" in which God is said to repeat the eternal self-activation of his triune life *pro nobis* analogously in revelation is, Moltmann argues, a case in point of a position which, despite all efforts to the contrary, is finally more Platonic than trinitarian. "Despite all his polemic against Luther's distinction between the *Deus revelatus* and the *Deus absconditus* Barth himself again comes close to such a distinction."[39]

In rejecting the notions of "primary" and "secondary" objectivity it follows that the distinctions in classical forms of trinitarian thought between God's relations *ad intra* and *ad extra* must also be rejected. Christian theology, it is claimed, has no warrant on the basis of a biblical view of revelation for speaking of an ontological triunity *immanent* within the godhead which is distinguishable from an *economic* or dispensational triunity of God's relationships to the world. What happens in the cross of Jesus Christ is not a temporal symbol or a historical analogy of an eternal happening beyond this history within God; it *is* the history of God happening.

To develop such an ontological thesis Moltmann turns increasingly in *The Crucified God* away from what he has earlier defined exegetically as a process of the working of the word and draws more heavily upon Hegelian thought forms. Bloch's ontology of the "not-yet-being" is also still in the background, though not as explicitly dealt with as in the former discussion of God as Future. Even the categories of Whiteheadean process metaphysics, certainly the most prevalent metaphysical influence in contemporary American theology, are commented upon in a much more sympathetic light. Whereas previously Moltmann had dismissed such process theology for defining God's being as a "becoming God" from the standpoint of "the dynamics of the world process," rather than from the standpoint of revelation in the form of promise,[40] he now writes, "Understood in trinitarian terms, God both transcends the world and is immanent in history, as process theology says in the bipolar concept of God without trinitarian thought."[41] The intent of Moltmann in such an appropriation is to discover conceptual resources with which to explain the central theme in his discussion of the Trinity; namely, that "we take part in the trinitarian process of God's history."[42] One may even speak, therefore, with this point in view like the process theologians of "panentheism."[43]

The dogmatic task as Moltmann sets it, for which he draws upon these metaphysical theories of process, is to conceive of the triunity of God from the perspective of the self-differentiation and self-forsakenness revealed in the suffering of the cross. "The form of the crucified one is the Trinity."[44] The passion of Jesus is to be taken as an actual cry of God against God. "The Son suffers in his love the forsaking by the Father in his death. The Father suffers in his love the grief of the death of the Son. Whatever proceeds from the event between the Father and the Son must then be understood as the Spirit of the self-giving (*Hingabe*) of the Father and the Son, as the Spirit which creates love for forsaken human beings, as the Spirit which makes the dead live."[45] All human history may be said to be involved within this eschatological process of divine reality which stems from the cross of Christ. All the pain and joy of the world are taken up in the movement of this spirit. In this universal participation historical reality itself dialectically becomes the "materialization" and "sacrament" of the eschatological presence of God.[46] Understood in this manner, Moltmann concludes, "the doctrine of the trinity is then no longer an exorbitant and impractical speculation about God, but nothing other than a short version of the passion narrative of Christ in its significance for the eschatological freedom of faith and the life of oppressed nature."[47]

It is quite plain, however, that in developing this ontological description of God as Triune Moltmann's claims have exceeded those positions which can be established by appealing to revelation as a promissory "passion narrative of Christ." The forms of process metaphysics appropriated in this description, whether from Hegel, from Bloch, or from Whitehead, are not commensurate with the idea of a process of the working of the word. Their fundamental notions originate from other contexts of thought. In subscribing to them the language of promise is no longer adhered to. It may be the case, of course, that the logic of a theory of promissory revelation does not lend itself to a doctrine of the Trinity, that the ideas of eternity as futurity, of divine transcendence and immanence as imminence, of God's promissory presence as *Selbigkeit,* make a contemporary understanding of this doctrine impossible. But let us see what claims, however limited, are warranted in this regard.

Any attempt to think of God horizontally rather than vertically and to equate God's very being univocally with a historical occurrence, the cross under Pilate, runs the risk of confusing God with the world, the Creator with creation. Pantheistic religion may welcome such an equation, but the Old and New Testaments reject it as a confusion and a distortion of reality. A main purpose of trinitarian doctrine in the Christian tradition has been to safeguard the conviction that in Jesus of Nazareth God identifies *with* the world in such a way that the world cannot be identified *as* God.

In this connection we do well to recall why Barth believed it necessary to follow the Cappadocians of the fourth century in insisting upon an immanent as well as an economic Trinity. The issue with Barth, from the beginning of his critical reaction to the liberal Protestantism of the nineteenth century, is one of avoiding any hint of confusing the Creator with the creature. His reasons had to do with political consequences, not only with academic theology. The world is not to be identified as God. The deification of any human state of affairs leads to its dehumanization. "A Trinity of *being,* not just an economic Trinity," as Barth wrote to his friend Thurneysen, is judged by Barth to be essential in preventing such an idolatrous identification.[48] Unless God and the world are clearly seen to be ontologically distinct, the meaning of a relationship of commitment between them established solely on the basis of a free decision and of love is lost. That which is necessary because of nature is not something which is constituted by a promise. The relation of covenant with creation which God elects is not the relation of Siamese twins. If God freely elects to have a world and relate to it, then God cannot be presumed to be dependent upon a world in order to be God.

Furthermore, to hold that God is relational only vis-à-vis the world, in Barth's view, would be to imply either that the world is of necessity God (and thus righteous!), or that God's own being as we know it is not a relationality of love in freedom. "It is not as though God stands in need of another as His partner, and in particular of man, in order to be truly God. . . . Why should God not also be able, as eternal Love, to be sufficient unto Himself? In His life as Father, Son, and Holy Spirit He would in truth be no lonesome, no egotistical God even without man, yes, even without the whole created universe."[49] With this conception of an immanent as well as economic Trinity one can furthermore accommodate the belief, expressed in various ways throughout Christian history, that in the final consummation of all things the mode of dispensation of God's grace, the divine economy, changes, but the eternal being of that grace as loving relationality remains constant. From this argument we may observe three principles which, in Barth's reasoning, are essential to Christian thought and which a doctrine of the immanent Trinity serves to maintain. 1) There is an absolute ontological distinction between God and the world. 2) There is a threefold relationality of God revealed to the world which is not dependent upon the world. 3) This relationality is eternal and irrevocable even though the mode of its dispensation to the world changes in the final consummation.

Moltmann for his part does not reject the idea of an immanent or ontological Trinity. Quite to the contrary, he affirms as does Barth a Trinity of being, but unlike Barth he equates this being with the economy of God's work in history.[50] This he believes is demanded by an incarnational theology of the cross. The aim is to develop an ontological description of the inner life of God from the history of Jesus Christ, understood now not as a "fixed and presupposed" reality, but as a "parable open to the eschaton."[51] It is with the christological identification of God, with the historical and eschatological way in which God may be said to identify with the world *sub Pontio Pilato,* that

Moltmann is most concerned in delineating the ontological character of ultimate reality. If we question Moltmann's line of reasoning on each of Barth's three points the results would appear to be as follows.

1) The ontological distinction between God and the world is to be interpreted as a temporal distinction between the imminence of the future and all that now is or has been. This is necessary if the horizontal perspective of biblical eschatology is not to be ignored. On the one hand Moltmann writes that this temporal category of the future belongs to the reality of God. From this statement it would appear to follow that the divine imminence is to be accorded an ultimate ontological status. The word "being" when properly understood with reference to God means "coming." On the other hand, however, we are told that this temporal distinction will come to an end in the final consummation when the glory of God's "eternal presence" will take place, "ontologically speaking," in that "being and nonbeing are no longer intertwined."[52] From this statement it would appear that the divine imminence is not to be accorded an ultimate ontological status, that eternity does not mean futurity. In the new creation, unlike in the old where "being and nonbeing are intertwined," the process of God's working will come to rest. One may sum up this ontological vision by saying that whereas now God is to come, in the consummation God comes to be. The question which must be put to Moltmann, however, is whether this new creative act on the part of God entails a change within God's own being, with the result that the imminence no longer remains a characteristic of God and the distinction between Creator and creature is no more, or whether God truly is as revealed.

2) With regard to the second proposition, that there is a threefold relationality of God revealed to the world which is not dependent upon the world, Moltmann's thesis is that this threefold relationality of God is not simply disclosed by the crucifixion of Christ; it happens in this crucifixion. The abandonment of the Son by the Father in a Spirit of mutual surrender on the cross requires that a christological understanding of ultimate reality be formulated in trinitarian terms. In this instance the relationality is not one of God as unitary *monarchia* in relation to the world (or of bi-polar deity in relation to the world!) but rather of God as a triune process of relationality extending out from the suffering of the cross through history to incorporate the world and

thereby in this Spirit make all things new. To say that the Trinity is constituted by the crucifixion is to say that God as eschatological process shapes the past, the present, and the future of the world in this cruciform—and thereby relational as self-confronting—manner from this historical locus. By this description it would appear that Moltmann seeks to correct any earlier Sabellian implications in his concept of God as Future to the effect that the three persons of the godhead are to be conceived in periodic sequence and to make this correction, at the same time, without forfeiting the horizontal and historical perspective which this reference to the future affords. But here again, as we have seen, two claims remain in tension. The crucifixion, we are told, is not to be interpreted along the lines of Hegel's "speculative Good Friday" as a timeless element within an immanent divine process of world reality. Yet this crucifixion is interpreted by Moltmann as death "within God" who as an eschatological process is said "panentheistically" to contain through this death in his inner trinitarian life all the godforsakenness, suffering, and death of the world.

3) On the third matter it is plainly stated in Moltmann's description that the triune relationality cannot be separated from the mode of its revealed dispensation to the world. In this respect God is his economy. Hence we must conclude that if the character of this divine economy is held to change in the final consummation, then there are no grounds in revelation for saying that God is an eternal Trinity. Not only does God ultimately cease to be Future, and Person, and Crucified; God also ceases to be Triune. We cannot even say that God's true selfhood has been revealed. This calls for clarification of what exactly the logic of Moltmann's theory of revelation does entail.

If we restrict ourselves to the claims which Moltmann makes for revelation in the language of promise, and leave aside the metaphysical notions of process which cannot be shown to derive from the logic of this language, we arrive at the fundamental affirmation of Moltmann's theory, that God the Promisor promises to be present. Moltmann elaborates this rudimentary description of God in a variety of ways, using both biblical and nonbiblical terminology, as his ontological proposals attest, but it remains at base the one essential characterization of God which his theory propounds. Our analysis of the speech-act of promising in ordinary discourse, and of the role of narrative in creating

historical significance, has been directed toward an intelligible understanding of this basic faith assertion. Now we must attempt to judge
the extent to which this assertion lends itself to a trinitarian formulation. Can it be so interpreted eschatologically, with reference to
history, in a manner which is not Sabellian?[53]

The starting point in Moltmann's view of revelation is the fact of the
promise itself. In revelation we have to do always with a particular story
told of a people Israel which culminates in an account of the life, death,
and destiny of Jesus of Nazareth. The reality designated by the name
and title "Jesus Christ" is not available to us apart from this story.
When heard in faith the primary significance of this narration—for it is
an ongoing telling—becomes that of a promise of God's own faithfulness with regard to all present and future events. Insofar as the verb
"promises" in the summary statement, God the Promisor *promises* to
be present, is interpreted as denoting the act of revelation that occurs in
Jesus Christ as promissory narration, this term in traditional trinitarian
language must be identified as the Son. Disclosed in the act of promising as "constitutive facts," to borrow the analytical label, is the self-
involvement of a promisor and the relation to the future which are
presented—made present—by this act. Unless we can say this with
reference to revelatory language, as well as to ordinary discourse, we
cannot say that an actual promise has occurred. Thus from the givenness
of the promising, or to state the point theologically, from the
revelation in the Son, it is conceptually coherent to speak of a promisor
(the Father) and of a presence (the Holy Spirit) without resorting to
extraneous mythological hypostatizations. Through Jesus Christ, who as
promissory narration manifests both historical and eschatological
significance (the Son), the promisor (the Father) is presented (the
Spirit) as committed to a future. The relation of Father, Son, and Spirit,
when conceived as that of the Promisor, the Promise, and the Presence,
is, therefore, neither sequential nor timeless. It is not sequential
because the promissory narration concerning Jesus Christ (the Son), the
self-involvement of the promisor for the future (the Father), and the
presence that is instituted by this language-event and that is the expression of it (the Spirit) each involves the others in its occurrence, yet
none is replaceable by the others. It is not timeless because promissory
presence involves a commitment to the future which as a divine con-

stancy submits to no abrogation, and promissory narration discloses that this future is not abstract futurity, but the future of one crucified under Pontius Pilate, whose story of universal promise provides the narrative means necessary for the historical significance of all things and renders the divine constancy as history.[54]

We may recognize, therefore, that an adherence to the basic claims in Moltmann's theory of revelation entails that the ontological descriptions of God as Future, as Person, as Crucified, and as Triune must be developed in harmony with the understanding of God's reality in Jesus Christ as promissory narration. When this is done, God's triune being can, as Moltmann insists it must, be affirmed as God's historical economy without concluding, as Moltmann clearly tends at some points in his argument to suggest, that God's own being essentially changes in the final consummation. Fulfillment is not to be conceived either as everlasting *chronos* or as an abrogation and cessation of promise. It cannot mean the end of God the Promisor promising his presence. It can mean a "glorification," as Moltmann himself says, preferring this expression to "fulfillment," in which the kingdom is established.[55] But the new creation is not absorbed into God so that all distinction between Creator and creature is lost because God's eternal presence is not all consuming, but constantly self-covenanting and promissory, as revealed.[56] It is metaphysical idealism which confuses covenantal unity with a spiritual process of unification.[57] One may with consistency agree with a characteristic statement of Moltmann such as the following— "His future is our presence, and his presence will be our future"[58]— only if the presence referred to in each instance is understood to be promissory.

This brief restatement of what I take to be the inherent logic of Moltmann's basic claims presents a somewhat different line of reasoning from his own more expansive language of metaphysical process. Obviously many ontological problems remain. Yet within the limits set by a theory of revelation in the language of promise (and that is our sole concern) this restatement is not necessarily irreconcilable with Moltmann's explicit conclusions. Even in according ultimate ontological status to God's eschatological reality as promise, the point at which Moltmann's own position would appear to differ the most, we may point out that there are sections in his writings that at least raise the possibility of maintaining a similar view. With one of them I will conclude this discussion of God's being.

> When finally everything shall come to pass and God himself comes, when his presence changes the ontic condition of all things and relationships, then the interpretation of the scriptural promise will take place not only for the salvation and the freedom of mankind but for the coming glory of God himself. Then it will also be a doxology, to be sure, here in the form of calling out of the depths, but still a doxology, the proclamation of God for God's own sake.[59]

PROMISE AND WORLD-OPENNESS

If the interpretation is correct that the basic ontological description of God's reality which results from the logic of Moltmann's theory of revelation is that God the Promisor promises to be present, what correlative understanding of world reality as a historical process may then be said to be coherent with this description?

Moltmann makes two primary claims in this regard. The first is that world reality, the entire realm of creation, becomes a historical process *through* the working of revelation. As the "apocalypse of the promised future," and not as an "epiphany of eternal presence," revelation is to be conceived as the opening up of the cosmos and of the human self to the future of God's truth. Apart from this revelatory activity of God such eschatological world-openness does not occur. This is the first insistence. The second is that world reality as historical process comes to an end.

As Moltmann elaborates his first claim his discussion exhibits the equivocal stance which we have detected in his theory from the outset. The conceptuality which is appropriated to develop the exegetical position that revelation is eschatological and promissory is in crucial instances incompatible with this position. This incompatibility can be clearly seen, for example, in Moltmann's statement that the cosmos, as well as the human self, shares in the *cor inquietum*.[60] "To man's 'restless heart' (Augustine) there corresponds a 'restless world.' "[61] Here, we face the problem of the ambiguity of Moltmann's theory in reference to the *cor inquietum* issue. When relying upon Blochian ontological conceptions which are not derived from an analysis of promissory language, statements are made concerning reality as a historical process such as the following: "We can therefore rediscover in the intentions and tendencies of all beings in history something of what is called in traditional language 'spirit.' It is the agony, the motivating force, the tension of matter."[62] From assertions of this sort one might conclude that the "restless world" is but the world process itself, apart from any promissory revelation of God, portrayed along the lines of Bloch's ontology of "not-yet-being." But elsewhere, in distinguishing his own view from that of Bloch, Moltmann can say that Christian hope "has its ground, not in the open possibilities of the world process, but solely in that which has come to the fore in the resurrection as God's possibility."[63] What has thus "come to the fore" is designated as God's "promise," and it is then argued that the co-called "open possibilities of the world process" are created by this promise. Thus in this connection we read: "The Augustinian *cor inquietum* is not a universal human presupposition for the Christian understanding of God, but rather it is the identifying mark of God's pilgrim people and the aim of the Christian mission to all men. It is only in the biblical understanding of God that human existence experiences itself as being moved by the question of God."[64]

A clarification of the relation of promise to process, it may be remarked parenthetically, would appear to be essential to the working out of any eschatological ontology which seeks to be governed by a Pauline vision of creation as "travail."[65] Whether it be with Sarah, the mother of Isaac, that first "child of promise," or with Mary, the mother of Jesus, in whom "all the promises of God find their confirmation," the birth pangs which each endured are depicted in the scriptural narratives as dependent upon God's promise.[66]

The theoretical difficulty arises, of course, in moving from myth to metaphysics, or, more exactly, in moving from exegesis to dogmatics by way of the move from promissory language to ontological claims concerning world process. We must at this point respect Moltmann's characterization of such descriptions on his part as heuristic rather than scientific accounts. As we have seen, he prefers to speak of the world as historical process in the categories of mission rather than of metaphysics. "In the place of a metaphysics of universal history appears a mission aimed at the universal which is future and not yet present."[67] Nevertheless, as he himself acknowledges, ontological descriptions are unavoidably implicit in this kind of talk of mission (*Sendung*) and cannot be ignored.[68] History is depicted both as a mode of consciousness and as a mode of being.

Moltmann's second primary claim regarding the process of world reality as history is that this process comes to an end. There is to be envisioned a fulfillment in which God will be "all in all."[69] This new creation is not, as we have already discussed, interpreted by Moltmann as simply a restoration of God's original order of creation. "It was exactly the apocalyptic theology of the New Testament which developed that knowledge of the new which is not only new as compared with sin, but also as compared with creation. In Christian theology this knowledge was preserved by Irenaeus (*imago Dei-similitudo Dei*), Athanasius (*theopoiesis*), Augustine (*non posse peccare, non posse mori*), Osiander, and Karl Barth."[70] The recognition of this still outstanding future is necessary, in Moltmann's judgment, if theology is to avoid the error of some romanticist positions of making pantheistic equations between the present world as a developing process and God. Thus one must in the Christian context speak of an end of the historical world process, caught up as this process is in "the difference between existence and essence."[71] "The openness of Christian existence," Moltmann writes, "comes to an end, for it is not openness for a future which remains empty, but rather it has the future of Christ for its presupposition and finds in it its fulfillment."[72]

In light of our discussion of according an ultimate ontological status to God's own reality as promise we must now ask if the claim that world reality as a historical process comes to an end entails as well the thesis that God's *promissory* being also comes to an end. Here the ambiguity in Moltmann's argument becomes most apparent. It can be illustrated by the following statement in which reference is made to the proclamation of the resurrection of the crucified Christ: "One can designate the still outstanding and yet to be cashed in significance of this event as *promissio* and say that the promise constantly outstrips the past of its well-being and first becomes transitory through fulfillment when it becomes clear that *the promise does not first lead toward the event,* but rather is nothing other than the *explication (Explikation)* of the eschatological openness of the event itself, which is only possible in this form."[73] The critical term here is "explication." What precisely does it mean in this sentence? If eschatological openness is the ultimate ontological category apart from promise, and *promissio* "does not first lead toward the event" but is only a "transitory" form of significance, then it is plainly illogical to say, as Moltmann does, that promises function in a performative manner in revelation and that as language-events they are integral to the future. Explication in this case would have to be conceived as illumination rather than initiation, thereby contradicting the fundamental difference which is initially drawn between "the hope-sentences of promise" and "descriptive sentences." If promise does not institute and constitute the divine presence of eschatological openness, of imminence, but is merely an expression of this openness which is no longer required in fulfillment, or in glory, then the whole objection to Platonic and two-level ways of thinking collapses, and Moltmann's critique of such thinking which runs throughout all his discussion of revelation is undercut.

To prevent this self-contradiction one must, it seems to me, follow the lead instead of other statements in Moltmann's theology which suggest that fulfillment is not the abrogation, and in this sense not the "end," of God's promise.[74] We may speak of a culmination of world reality in a new heaven and a new earth without violating the character of promissory significance. To be sure, this world as a present state of affairs cannot pantheistically be identified with God. It is not eternal, nor are its processes. In his discussion of narrative sentences Danto writes, " 'The Future is open' 'says only that nobody has written the history of the Present.' "[75] A Christian theology need not agree that this is *all* that the statement, "The Future is open," says, but it can agree that this is part. As long as God is understood to be revealed as the Promisor who promises to be present there will be a story waiting to be told. How that story will develop we do not know. The promise is that all stories shall ultimately become a part of the one story in which the life, death, and destiny of Jesus of Nazareth will be the integrative theme. In this sense the historical significance arising from promissory narration may be said to remain even though the present process of world reality as history is held to come to an end in a new creation of being. One need not be equivocal about ascribing ultimate status to the promise of God, either with respect to an ontology of God's own being, or with respect to an ontology of the being of God's creation. A theory of revelation developed in harmony with the concepts of promise and narration cannot intelligibly do otherwise.

THE LOGIC OF PROMISSORY NARRATION

In conclusion there remains to be assessed the requirement of intelligibility itself in Moltmann's theory of revelation. We have observed that the very intention, as Moltmann has stated it, "to develop an understanding of the 'revelation of God' that is eschatological insofar as it attempts to uncover the language of promise" involves an initial assumption that revelation exhibits a form of significance which can be "uncovered." We have further seen that one of the requirements for producing such a theological "understanding" is that a reasoned account of the conditions for the meaning and truth of the claims which are made must be developed in conjunction with other sciences. The privileged and unsupported assertions of a "revelational positivism" are to be rejected. If this rejection is consistently maintained it follows that the uncovering of promissory significance is a matter not only of exegesis, but also of logic. To recall a statement of Gerhard Sauter referred to at the beginning, "Whoever takes as his starting point the category of 'promise' must proceed to the working out of a theological logic."[76]

Such a logic, I have argued, if it is to give due regard both to the linguistic and historical character of revelation, as Moltmann insists, involves an analysis of promissory narration as the basic form in which the revelatory message of the Christian mission comes to expression. Revelation itself is not dependent upon such reasoning, but a theological understanding of revelation is. The intelligibility is necessary for the practice of the Christian mission. *Fides quaerens intellectum* is in essence *promissio quaerens missionem*. This intelligibility, Moltmann acknowledges, is finally subject only to an eschatological verification. It must, however, be governed by the language and history of promise and continually examined in this regard.

The ontological claims which result from a logic of promissory narration arise from the commitments which are implicit in such language—self-involvement, a relation to the future, the role of narrative in creating historical significance. To be consistent with Moltmann's critique of Barth's "transcendentalism," I have contended, the terms "promise" and "narrative" when applied to revelation must be said to retain their ordinary meaning.[77] A description of God's being based upon this meaning, as any other ontological or formal description, does not deal with the material content of who God is. It does explain why talk of an eschatological and historical "Who" from the standpoint of Christian revelation is appropriate.

With the exception of Evans the analytical philosophers whom we have consulted have not, of course, explicitly been addressing theological problems. There is a conceptual sobriety in the reality claims which they are willing to allow. In writing about the problem of reference as naming, for example, Searle cautions against "the metaphysical mistake of deriving ontological conclusions from linguistic theses." The "original sin of all metaphysics," he writes, is "the attempt to read real or alleged features of language into the world."[78] Yet with respect precisely to the self-involvement manifest in speech-acts Searle concludes that "there is no separating those speech acts from the commitments which form essential parts of them."[79] Furthermore, in answer to Searle, it must be added that his own (metaphysical?) notion of "world" in the above statement is not that of the world as history. A historical world does not exist apart from language, as the discussion of narrative by Gallie and Danto makes plain. "Analysis, in short," Danto writes, "yields a descriptive metaphysics when systematically executed."[80]

The very sobriety of the analytical approach in the area of ontology, however, may not itself be inimical to an eschatological vision of reality. A contemporary revival of the principle of parsimony in systematic theology may even be supported as salutary if such a principle serves not to domesticate grace and to trivialize mystery, but, on the contrary, to prevent the christening of muddles as mysteries. What is lost in metaphysical postulation is gained in theological accountability and coherence. The logic of promissory narration does not yield an extensive ontology. It does, I have sought to show, make understandable the one ontological description of God most central in Moltmann's theory of revelation. God the Promisor promises to be present in all the affairs of life, and death, and destiny in the manner of the Crucified and Risen Christ. There are those whose lives attest that this is a confidence sufficient in which to live and die.

ABBREVIATIONS

CG   Jürgen Moltmann, *The Crucified God: The Cross of Christ as the Foundation and Criticism of Christian Theology*, trans. R.A. Wilson and John Bowden (New York: Harper and Row, 1974).

CJT   *Canadian Journal of Theology*

CS   Jürgen Moltmann, *The Church in the Power of the Spirit: A Contribution to Messianic Ecclesiology*, trans. Margaret Kohl (New York: Harper and Row, 1977).

HeyJ   *Heythrop Journal*

HP   Jürgen Moltmann, *Hope and Planning*, trans. Margaret Clarkson (New York: Harper and Row, 1971).

PhRev *Philosophical Review*

PT   Jürgen Moltmann, *Perspektiven der Theologie: Gesammelte Aufsätze* (Munich: Chr. Kaiser Verlag, 1968).

RRF   Jürgen Moltmann, *Religion, Revolution, and the Future*, trans. M. Douglas Meeks (New York: Charles Scribner's Sons, 1969).

SBT   Studies in Biblical Theology

TH   Jürgen Moltmann, *Theology of Hope: On the Ground and the Implications of a Christian Eschatology*, trans. James W. Leitch (New York: Harper and Row, 1967).

USQR *Union Seminary Quarterly Review*

WA   Martin Luther, Kritische Gesamtausgabe (Weimar)

NOTES

CHAPTER I

1. Jürgen Moltmann, *Theology of Hope: On the Ground and the Implications of a Christian Eschatology,* trans. James W. Leitch (New York: Harper & Row, 1967), p. 42, (p. 35). Hereafter referred to as *TH.* Throughout this essay in citations of Moltmann's works the numbers in parentheses indicate the pages in the original German texts, here *Theologie der Hoffnung: Untersuchungen zur Begründung und zu den Konsequenzen einer christlichen Eschatologie* (Munich: Chr. Kaiser Verlag, 1964). I have altered the English translations whenever it seemed to me that a more exact rendering of the original could be made.

2. See, for example, J.L. Austin, *How to Do Things with Words,* ed. J.O. Urmson (Cambridge: Harvard University Press, 1962); Donald D. Evans, *The Logic of Self-Involvement: A Philosophical Study of Everyday Language with Special Reference to the Christian Use of Language about God as Creator* (London: SCM Press, 1963); Robert W. Jenson, *The Knowledge of Things Hoped For: The Sense of Theological Discourse* (New York: Oxford University Press, 1969); John R. Searle, *Speech Acts: An Essay in the Philosophy of Language* (London: Cambridge University Press, 1969). Journal articles pertaining to this subject are numerous.

3. Pannenberg, Sauter, and Moltmann are discussed by James M. Robinson in *Theology as History,* vol. 3, *New Frontiers in Theology,* eds. James M. Robinson and John B. Cobb, Jr. (New York: Harper & Row, 1967), pp. 1-100, and by Klaus Koch in *The Rediscovery of Apocalyptic,* vol. 22, *SBT* 2d ser. (Naperville: Alec R. Allenson, Inc., 1975), pp. 98–111. For a discussion of Metz and Moltmann see Walter H. Capps, *Time Invades the Cathedral: Tensions in the School of Hope*

(Philadelphia: Fortress Press, 1972), pp. 41–90. On the background of hope theology see especially Merrill Douglas Meeks, *Origins of the Theology of Hope* (Philadelphia: Fortress Press, 1974).

4. Wolfhart Pannenberg, *Basic Questions in Theology,* trans. George H. Kehm, I (Philadelphia: Fortress Press, 1970), pp. 15–80.

5. Ibid., p. 19.

6. Ibid., p. 21.

7. Wolfhart Pannenberg et al., *Revelation as History,* trans. David Granskou (New York: Macmillan Company, 1968). Pannenberg refers to this change in his position in *Basic Questions in Theology,* I, xvii and in *Theology as History,* eds. James M. Robinson and John B. Cobb, Jr., pp. 258–260.

8. Gerhard Sauter, *Zukunft und Verheissung: Das Problem der Zukunft in der gegenwärtigen theologischen und philosophischen Diskussion* (Zurich: Zwingli Verlag, 1965).

9. Ibid., p. 20.

10. Ibid., p. 70.

11. Ibid., pp. 149ff.

12. Gerhard Sauter, *Erwartung und Erfahrung* (Munich: Chr. Kaiser Verlag, 1972), pp. 287–288.

13. See Johannes B. Metz, *Theology of the World,* trans. William Glen-Doepel (New York: Herder and Herder, 1971).

14. Ibid., p. 87.

15. Ibid., p. 89.

16. Johannes B. Metz, "The Future in the Memory of Suffering," *New Questions on God,* ed. Johannes B. Metz, *Concilium,* no. 76 (New York: Herder and Herder, 1972), p. 19.

17. Metz, *Theology of the World,* pp. 107ff.

18. Rudolf Bultmann, *Jesus Christ and Mythology* (New York: Charles Scribner's Sons, 1958), p. 13. It is interesting to note a contemporary parallel to Kaftan's statement, as cited here by Bultmann, in the following assertion by Walter Capps: "There is a fundamental error in the assumption that a theology that draws man's attention to the future can use that perspective as the schema for setting forth a correct summary of Christian belief. If theology must always be normative, that is, if it must make biblical teaching and the articles of faith subject to a systematic principle, it really cannot be a theology of the future or a

theology of hope." (*Time Invades the Cathedral*, p. 143.) My question is, can it be a theology of promise?

19. Adolf Harnack, *What is Christianity?*, trans. Thomas Bailey Saunders (New York: Harper & Brothers, 1957), p. 56. These lectures were delivered by Harnack at Berlin in 1899–1900.

20. Johannes Weiss, *Jesus' Proclamation of the Kingdom of God*, Lives of Jesus Series, eds. and trans. Richard H. Hiers and D. Larrimore Holland (Philadelphia: Fortress Press, 1971), p. 135.

21. For Barth's indebtedness to the Blumhardts, father and son, see his article, "Past and Future: Friedrich Naumann and Christoph Blumhardt" (1919), *The Beginnings of Dialectic Theology*, ed. James M. Robinson, trans. Keith R. Crim and Louis De Grazia (Richmond: John Knox Press, 1968), pp. 35–45. "To believe in 'God' meant, for the two Blumhardts, to take this comprehensive hope seriously, more seriously than all other considerations . . . This new insight is all along the line and in all points down to the present day a total contrast to the general religion of churches and pastors of all denominations" (p. 42).

22. Karl Barth, *Theology and Church*, trans. Louise P. Smith (New York: Harper & Row, 1962) pp. 55–73.

23. Ibid., p. 61.

24. Ibid., p. 73.

25. Karl Barth, *The Epistle to the Romans*, trans. Edwyn C. Hoskyns (6th ed.; London: Oxford University Press, 1933), p. 314.

26. For Barth's later estimate of Overbeck and his revised opinion of the place of eschatology in dogmatics see Karl Barth, *Church Dogmatics, The Doctrine of the Word of God*, vol. 1, pt. 2, trans. G.T. Thomson and Harold Knight (Edinburgh: T. & T. Clark, 1956), pp. 58 and 876, and particularly *Church Dogmatics, The Doctrine of God*, vol. 2, pt. 1, trans. T. H. L. Parker, W.B. Johnston, Harold Knight, J. L. M. Haire (Edinburgh: T. & T. Clark, 1957), pp. 608–677.

27. See, for example, Rudolf Bultmann, *History and Eschatology* (Edinburgh: University Press, 1957), pp. 151–155, and Karl Barth, *Church Dogmatics* vol. 1, pt. 2, pp. 45–121.

28. Rudolf Bultmann, *History and Eschatology*, pp. 149–155.

29. Karl Barth, *Church Dogmatics*, vol. 1, pt. 2, pp. 45–70 and vol. 2, pt. 1, pp. 608–677.

30. It should be observed that the questions Metz puts to Rahner are

similar to those put to the dialectical theologians: ". . . Does not a radical transcendental-existential theology undervalue the rank of eschatology? Can the eschatology really be extrapolated out of the existential approach of theology? Or does not every anthropocentrically oriented theology which does not want to leave the world and history out of sight of operative and responsible faith flow into an eschatologically oriented theology?" See "Foreword" by Johannes B. Metz in Karl Rahner's *Spirit in the World,* trans. William Dych (London: Sheed and Ward, 1968), p. xviii.

31. Klaus Koch, *The Rediscovery of Apocalyptic*, pp. 13–17.

32. Rudolf Bultmann, "The Significance of the Old Testament for the Christian Faith," *The Old Testament and Christian Faith: A Theological Discussion,* ed. Bernhard W. Anderson (New York: Harper & Row, 1963), p. 35.

33. Rudolf Bultmann, "Prophecy and Fulfillment," *Essays on Old Testament Hermeneutics,* ed. Claus Westermann (Richmond: John Knox Press, 1963), pp. 50–75.

34. Ibid., p. 73.

35. See the essay by Zimmerli, "Promise and Fulfillment," *Essays on Old Testament Hermeneutics,* ed. Claus Westermann, pp. 89–122, especially p. 119.

36. Ibid., pp. 111–112.

37. Ibid., p. 120.

38. Gerhard von Rad, *Old Testament Theology,* trans. D. M. G. Stalker, vol. 1 (New York: Harper & Row, 1962), particularly pp. 167–175.

39. Ibid., p. 106.

40. Ibid., p. 116.

41. Ibid., p. 170.

42. Rolf Rendtorff, "The Concept of Revelation in Ancient Israel," *Revelation as History,* ed. Wolfhart Pannenberg, p. 47.

43. For critical responses to Käsemann's thesis see *Apocalypticism,* vol. 6, *Journal for Theology and the Church,* ed. Robert W. Funk (New York: Herder and Herder, 1969).

44. Ernst Käsemann, *New Testament Questions of Today,* trans. W.J. Montague (Philadelphia: Fortress Press, 1969), p. 102.

45. Ibid., p. 109, n. 1.

46. Ibid., p. 86.

47. Ibid., p. 177.

48. Ibid., p. 181.

49. Ulrich Wilkens, "The Understanding of Revelation within the History of Primitive Christianity," *Revelation as History*, ed. Wolfhart Pannenberg, p. 111.

50. Ibid., p. 112.

51. For discussions of Bloch's contribution to theology see Francis P. Fiorenza, "Dialectical Theology and Hope," *HeyJ* 9 and 10 (1968–1969) and Walter Capps, *Time Invades the Cathedral*, pp. 15–40.

52. Jürgen Moltmann, "What is 'New' in Christianity: The Category *Novum* in Christian Theology," *Religion, Revolution, and the Future*, trans. M. Douglas Meeks (New York: Charles Scribner's Sons, 1969), p. 15. Hereafter referred to as *RRF*. This essay is not the same as the original "Die Kategorie *Novum* in der Christlichen Theologie" which appears in *Perspektiven der Theologie: Gesammelte Aufsätze* (Munich: Chr. Kaiser Verlag, 1968), pp. 174–188. Hereafter referred to as *PT*.

53. Jürgen Moltmann, "Introduction" to Ernst Bloch's *Man on His Own: Essays in the Philosophy of Religion*, trans. E.B. Ashton (New York: Herder and Herder, 1970), p. 20.

54. Jürgen Moltmann, *Theologie der Hoffnung*, pp. 313–334. English translation appears in *RRF*, pp. 148–176. Bloch's *Das Princip Hoffnung* (Frankfurt: Suhrkamp Verlag, 1959) was written during 1938–1947 while he was an exile in the United States and later revised in 1953 and 1959.

55. S. Unseld, ed., *Ernst Bloch zu ehren* (Frankfurt: Suhrkamp Verlage, 1965).

56. Gerhard Sauter, *Zukunft und Verheissung*, pp. 277–354.

57. For a biblical theologian's response to Bloch see Walther Zimmerli, *Man and His Hope in the Old Testament* (London: SCM Press, 1971), pp. 151–165.

58. Ernst Bloch, *Thomas Münzer als Theologie der Revolution* (Frankfurt: Suhrkamp Verlag, 1969), first published in 1921.

59. Note especially the writings in the philosophy of religion contained in *Man on His Own*, previously cited, and in *Atheism in*

Christianity: The Religion of the Exodus and the Kingdom, trans. J.T. Swann (New York: Herder and Herder, 1972).

60. Ernst Bloch, *Das Princip Hoffnung,* p. 592. Trans. in *Man on His Own,* p. 135.

61. Ernst Bloch, *Atheism in Christianity,* p. 265.

62. Ernst Bloch, *Das Princip Hoffnung,* p. 124.

63. Ibid., p. 10, also pp. 56ff.

64. Ibid., "Das Antizipierende Bewusstsein," the Second Part of five parts comprising *Das Princip Hoffnung,* pp. 49–391.

65. Ibid., pp. 129–203.

66. Ibid., p. 357, also Ernst Bloch, *Zur Ontologie des Noch-Nicht Seins* (Frankfurt: Suhrkamp Verlag, 1961), p. 17.

67. Ibid., p. 258.

68. Ibid., p. 1628.

69. See Roger Garaudy, *From Anathema to Dialogue,* trans. Luke O'Neill (New York: Herder and Herder, 1966); also these essays by Moltmann, "The Revolution of Freedom," *PT,* pp. 189–211 (somewhat altered in translation, *RRF,* pp. 63–82), and "Hope without Faith: An Eschatological Humanism without God," *Is God Dead?,* ed. Johannes B. Metz, *Concilium,* no. 16 (New York: Paulist Press, 1966), pp. 25–40.

70. See Gerhard Sauter, "The Future: A Question for the Christian-Marxist Dialogue," *The Problem of Eschatology,* ed. Edward Schillebeeckx and Boniface Willems, *Concilium,* no. 41 (New York: Paulist Press, 1969), pp. 125–134.

71. Jürgen Moltmann, *RRF,* pp. 200–201.

72. Ibid., p. 3. More recently Moltmann has objected to speculative discussions about the future, preferring to deal with the socio-political question, "Whose future?" Note his comments in *Hope and the Future of Man,* ed. Ewert H. Cousins (Philadelphia: Fortress Press, 1972), pp. 55–59. The significance of the future, however, remains.

73. Johannes B. Metz, *Theology of the World,* p. 73.

74. Wolfhart Pannenberg, "Der Gott der Hoffnung," *Ernst Bloch zu ehren,* ed. S. Unseld, pp. 209–225.

75. Wolfhart Pannenberg, *The Idea of God and Human Freedom,* trans. R.A. Wilson (Philadelphia: Westminster Press, 1973), p. 109.

76. Pannenberg makes an opposite move from the American

"process theologians" at this point. While they deny omnipotence and omniscience to God in order to allow for human freedom, they, for the most part, follow Whitehead in maintaining that God is an "actual entity." Pannenberg denies the entity status but insists that no being could be God who could not be "the reality which determines everything" (ibid., p. 109).

77. Ibid., p. 110.

78. Jürgen Moltmann, "The Future as New Paradigm of Transcendence," *RRF,* pp. 177–199.

79. Jean Danielou, *From Shadows to Reality: Studies in the Biblical Typology of the Fathers,* trans. Dom Wulstan Hibberd (London: Burns and Oates, 1960).

80. This is not to overlook the fact that Origen puts great stress upon allegorical interpretation. Danielou provides a more detailed examination of the exegesis of Irenaeus and Origen in *A History of Early Christian Doctrine Before the Council of Nicaea,* vol. 2, *Gospel Message and Hellenistic Culture,* trans. John A. Baker (Philadelphia: Westminster Press, 1973), chaps. 9 and 12. On the question of whether Origen's thought should be described as eschatological and historical see the critique of Danielou on this point in John Meyendorff, *Christ in Eastern Thought* (Washington: Corpus Books, 1969), p. 35.

81. For a discussion of this future direction in typology and how it conflicts with mythical thinking see Wolfhart Pannenberg, "Myth in Biblical and Christian Tradition," *The Idea of God and Human Freedom,* pp. 59–66. Pannenberg does not, however, consider the difference between shadows and promises as forms of the prefigurations of reality.

82. James Preus, *From Shadow to Promise: Old Testament Interpretation from Augustine to the Young Luther* (Cambridge: Harvard University Press, 1969).

83. Augustine, *On Christian Doctrine,* trans. D.W. Robertson, Jr. (New York: Liberal Arts Press, 1958), Book Three, chaps. XXX-XXXVII, pp. 104–117.

84. The text with introduction may be found in F.C. Burkitt, *The Book of Rules of Tyconius* (Cambridge, England: University Press, 1894). "The sole reference to Tyconius' book," Burkitt writes, "independent of the review in *de Doctrina Christiana* is that by the author

of *de Prommissionibus*"—most likely, S. Prosper of Aquitaine in the fifth century, pp. xxiv. Also, p. xx.

85. Augustine, *On Christian Doctrine*, chap. XXXIII, p. 107.

86. Augustine, *On the Spirit and the Letter,* chap. XXXIV, italics mine. *Basic Writings of Saint Augustine,* ed. Whitney J. Oates and trans. P. Holmes, vol. 1 (New York: Random House, 1948), p. 487.

87. Ibid., chap. XLIX, p. 500.

88. Ibid., chap. XXXVI, pp. 488–489.

89. This translation is by Wilhelm Pauck in his introduction to *Luther: Lectures on Romans,* trans. Wilhelm Pauck, *The Library of Christian Classics,* vol. 15 (Philadelphia: Westminster Press, 1961), p. xxviii. The actual words, which have been variously translated are:

> Litera gesta docet
> quid credas allegoria
> moralis quid agas
> quo tendas anagogia.

90. James Preus, *From Shadow to Promise,* pp. 22–23, n. 29.

91. As quoted from Luther's works, WA 4.310.28–32, by Preus, ibid., p. 183.

92. Ibid., p. 254.

93. Ibid., p. 188.

94. Martin Luther, WA 56, 45, 15ff., as translated in *Luther: Lectures on Romans,* ed. Wilhelm Pauck, p. 147.

95. James Preus, op. cit., p. 256.

96. See above, p. 11.

97. James M. Robinson and John B. Cobb, Jr., eds., *Theology as History,* p. 227.

98. Jürgen Moltmann, *Hope and Planning,* trans. Margaret Clarkson (New York: Harper & Row, 1971), p. 15. Hereafter referred to as *HP* (*PT*, p. 25).

99. See James M. Robinson and John B. Cobb, Jr., eds., *The New Hermeneutic* (New York: Harper & Row, 1964).

100. Gerhard Ebeling, *Introduction to a Theological Theory of Language,* trans. R.A. Wilson (Philadelphia: Fortress Press, 1973), p. 186.

101. James A. Martin, Jr., *The New Dialogue Between Philosophy and Theology* (New York: Seabury Press, 1966).

102. See Hans-Dieter Bastian, "From the Word to the Words," trans. Reinhard Ulrich, *Theology of the Liberating Word,* ed. Frederick Herzog (New York: Abingdon Press, 1971), pp. 46–75; also, in the same volume, Eberhard Jüngel, "God—As a Word of Our Language," trans. Robert T. Osborn, pp. 25–45.

103. Aloys Grillmeier, *Christ in Christian Tradition: From the Apostolic Age to Chalcedon* (451), trans. J.S. Bowden (New York: Sheed and Ward, 1965), pp. 27, 30.

104. Paul Tillich, *Systematic Theology,* vol. 1 (Chicago: University of Chicago Press, 1951), p. 157.

105. Ibid., n. 9, p. 157.

106. This is not to say that Tillich's theology is completely antithetical to the eschatological theologies. For an attempt to work out a "theology of hope" more in line with Tillich see Carl E. Braaten, *The Future of God* (New York: Harper & Row, 1969).

107. Karl Barth, *Church Dogmatics, The Doctrine of Reconciliation,* vol. 4, pt. 1, trans. G.W. Bromiley (Edinburgh: T. & T. Clark, 1956), p. 52. On this point see also Wolfhart Pannenberg, *Jesus—God and Man,* trans. Lewis L. Wilkins and Duane A. Priebe (Philadelphia: Westminster Press, 1968), p. 394.

108. Karl Barth, *Church Dogmatics, The Doctrine of God,* vol. 2, pt. 1, p. 16.

109. Karl Barth, *Church Dogmatics, The Doctrine of the Word of God,* vol. 1, pt. 1, trans. G.T. Thomson (Edinburgh: T. & T. Clark, 1936), p. 364; also *The Doctrine of the Word of God,* vol. 1, pt. 2, pp. 10ff. In later sections of the *Church Dogmatics,* i.e., vol. 4, Barth treats Scripture's role in revelation, not so much as language which names, *corresponding* to a divine subject, but as narrative language *rendering* the identity of that subject. This point of difference, not taken into account by Moltmann in his critique of Barth, has been developed by Hans W. Frei and by David H. Kelsey. See Hans W. Frei, *The Identity of Jesus Christ* (Philadelphia: Fortress Press, 1975), and David H. Kelsey, *The Uses of Scripture in Recent Theology* (Philadelphia: Fortress Press, 1975), pp. 39–55. Kelsey briefly compares the positions of Frei, Barth, and Moltmann on the importance each attaches to the narrative form of Scripture. See pp. 54–55.

110. Karl Barth, *Church Dogmatics, The Doctrine of God,* vol. 2, pt. 1, p. 233.

111. Karl Barth, *Church Dogmatics, The Doctrine of the Word of God*, vol. 1, pt. 2, p. 52.

112. Jürgen Moltmann, *TH*, p. 115 (p. 105).

CHAPTER II

1. See Moltmann's response to the American "theologians of play," "Are There No Rules of the Game?", in Jürgen Moltmann, *Theology of Play* (New York: Harper and Row, 1972), pp. 111–113. The listing of his rules here is my own and is drawn from his writings in their entirety.

2. Jürgen Moltmann, *The Crucified God: The Cross of Christ as the Foundation and Criticism of Christian Theology*, trans. R.A. Wilson and John Bowden (New York: Harper & Row, 1974), pp. 7–31 (pp. 12–33). Hereafter referred to as *CG*. The numbers here in parentheses indicate the pages in: *Der Gekreuzigte Gott: Das Kreuz Christi als Grund und Kritik christlicher Theologie* (Munich: Chr. Kaiser Verlag, 1972).

3. Jürgen Moltmann, "Theology as Eschatology," *The Future of Hope*, ed. Frederick Herzog (New York: Harper & Row, 1967), p. 1.

4. *RRF*, p. 203.

5. *HP*, p. 216 (*PT*, p. 284).

6. *CG*, p. 24 (p. 28).

7. *RRF*, pp. 203–204.

8. Jürgen Moltmann, "Theology as Eschatology," *The Future of Hope*, p. 8.

9. In this connection note especially the essays, "The Revelation of God and the Question of Truth" and "Theology in the World of Modern Science," in *HP*, pp. 3–30 and pp. 200–223 (*PT*, pp. 13–35 and 269–287).

10. *HP*, p. 3 (*PT*, p. 13).

11. *HP*, p. 215 (*PT*, p. 283).

12. *HP*, p. 216 (*PT*, p. 284).

13. *HP*, pp. 220–221 (*PT*, p. 287).

14. Jürgen Moltmann, "Towards the Next Step in the Dialogue," *The Future of Hope*, p. 157.

15. *RRF*, p. 102 (*PT*, p. 142).

16. *RRF*, p. 48.

17. *HP*, p. 206 (*PT*, p. 275).

18. *TH*, p. 272 (pp. 250–251).

19. *TH*, p. 65 (p. 57).

20. *RRF*, p. 207. In response to the criticism that his view of a *theologia viae* is noticeably lacking in "joy" (cf. Harvey Cox's criticism, for example, in "The Problem of Continuity," *The Future of Hope*, p. 80), Moltmann has more recently written: "On first glance *Christian theology* is indeed the *theory of a practice* which alleviates human need; the theory of preaching, of ministries and services. But on second glance Christian theology is also an abundant rejoicing in God and the *free play* of thoughts, words, images, and songs with the grace of God. In its one aspect it is the theory of a practice, in the other it is pure theory, i.e., a point of view which transforms the viewer into that which he views, hence *doxology.*" (*Theology of Play*, p. 27.) Is this a retraction of his original contrast between a *theologia viae* and a *theologia patriae*? I think not in light of the following statement from the conclusion of this same text: "When God will be 'all in all' we will be like those who dream. But we have not as yet reached that point. Only false prophets speak of peace when there is no peace and of total play when the great play has not even begun. The cross of Christ remains an offense, and Auschwitz remains Auschwitz—until the dead rise and all begin to dance because everything has become new. Until then there will be laughter underneath tears and tears within laughter" (ibid., p. 112).

21. *TH*, p. 57 (pp. 49–50).

22. John Macquarrie's comment in this regard is representative, "We need presence as well as promise." "Eschatology and Time," *The Future of Hope*, p. 123.

23. *TH*, p. 28 (p. 23).

24. *TH*, p. 29 (p. 24).

25. *HP*, p. 204 (*PT*, p. 273).

26. Matt. 4:14, Mark 1:15, Phil. 4:5.

27. *TH*, p. 84 (pp. 74–75).

28. *TH*, chap. 2, "Promise and History," pp. 95–138 (pp. 85–124).

29. Moltmann writes that the present mission of the Christian church must be seen "against the background of the Yahwist promise to Abraham." *TH*, p. 329 (pp. 303–304).

30. Gen. 17:17; 18:12.

31. *TH*, pp. 125–126 (p. 113).

32. *TH*, pp. 133ff. (pp. 120ff).

33. *TH*, p. 136 (p. 123).

34. Gerhard Von Rad, *Old Testament Theology*, trans. D. M. G. Stalker, vol. 2 (New York: Harper & Row, 1965), p. 371.

35. Moltmann's reading of Pauline theology is indebted to Ernst Käsemann. Hebrews is also a source here. The Gospel of John, on the other hand, is not cited in *TH*. Moltmann refers to it once for support in "Theology as Eschatology," *The Future of Hope*, p. 35. No emphasis is placed upon the teaching of Jesus.

36. 2 Cor. 1:20.

37. *TH*, p. 157 (p. 138). "Validation," as the English text translates it, misses the dynamic meaning intended. See also *CG*, p. 157 (p. 128, n. 47).

38. Gal. 4:28.

39. *TH*, pp. 179–180 (pp. 162–163).

40. On this point Moltmann differs with Zimmerli, whose judgment in Old Testament matters he tends to follow. Zimmerli writes, "But the new aspect of awaiting fulfillment is that fulfillment can bring nothing more than the open unveiling of that which is already fulfilled." ("Promise and Fulfillment," *Essays on Old Testament Hermeneutics*, ed. Claus Westermann, p. 114.)

41. *TH*, p. 163 (p. 148).

42. *RRF*, pp. 210–211.

43. *TH*, p. 17 (p. 13).

44. The translation of *Sätze* as "statements," as the English text has it, i.e., "doctrinal-statements" and "hope-statements," raises additional problems because of the more specialized meaning attached to "statements" in linguistic philosophy.

45. *TH*, p. 18 (pp. 13–14).

46. This translation is consistent with Moltmann's assertion elsewhere that "the promises are not descriptive words (*Deuteworte*) for the reality which is but action-words (*Tatworte*) in the expected occurrences of God's faithfulness." *TH*, p. 118 (p. 106).

47. *TH*, p. 18 (p. 14). The metaphors come from Kant.

48. *TH*, p. 75 (p. 66).

49. *TH*, p. 86 (p. 76).

50. Walter Capps, for example, writes concerning hope-theology: "On the more strictly philosophical side, its formal schematism has roots in the process-orientation of Heraclitus." ("An Assessment of the Theological Side of the School of Hope," *Cross Currents* 28, no. 3, 1968, 2d par., pages not numbered.)

51. For what follows see Jürgen Moltmann, "The Revelation of God and the Question of Truth," *HP*, pp. 3ff. (*PT*, pp. 13ff.).

52. *RRF*, p. 51. Moltmann acknowledges in a footnote that "I. M. Crombie and John Hick have spoken similarly of an 'eschatological verification' of God's existence." He does not, however, discuss their views. See *The Logic of God: Theology and Verification*, eds. Malcolm L. Diamond and Thomas V. Litzenburg, Jr. (Indianapolis: Bobbs-Merrill, 1975), pp. 181–243.

53. One is reminded here of Gabriel Marcel's definition of the prophetic character of hope as "a memory of the future." (*Homo Viator: Introduction to a Metaphysics of Hope*, trans. Emma Craufurd [Chicago: H. Regnery Company, 1951], p. 53.)

54. *TH*, p. 118 (p.106).

55. *HP*, p. 17 (*PT*, p. 27).

56. *TH*, p. 118 (pp. 106–107).

57. *TH*, p. 131 (p. 118).

58. *TH*, p. 202 (p. 184).

59. John Baillie, *The Idea of Revelation in Recent Thought* (New York: Columbia University Press, 1956), p. 47.

60. *TH*, p. 116 (pp.104–105).

61. *TH*, p. 40 (pp. 33–34).

62. *TH*, see esp. pp. 45ff. (pp. 38ff.).

63. *TH*, p. 52 (p. 44).

64. *TH*, p. 52 (p.45).

65. *TH*, p. 58 (p. 51).

66. Schleiermacher writes,"The doctrine of the Trinity is neither presupposed in every Christian religious experience nor contained in it. . . ." (*The Christian Faith*, trans. H.R. Mackintosh and J.S. Stewart [Edinburgh: T. & T. Clark, 1928], p. 144). He discusses the Trinity only at the "conclusion" of his dogmatics.

67. Karl Barth, "The Principles of Dogmatics According to Wilhelm Herrmann" (1925), *Theology and Church*, p. 256.

68. Loc. cit.

69. *TH*, p. 50 (p. 43).

70. *RRF*, p. 36.

71. Loc. cit.

72. *TH*, p. 229 (p. 209).

73. *TH*, pp. 115–116 (p. 104). The allusion here is to W. Zimmerli's interpretation of the Old Testament formula, "And they shall know that I am Yahweh," as a "self-presentation" formula to be understood as the naming of a person. Moltmann suggests that this explanation of revelation is in tension with the theological importance which Zimmerli himself attributes to promise, and on this point he sides with R. Rendtorff in holding that revelation has to do both with God's person and with his coming kingdom.

74. *TH*, p. 112 (p. 101).

75. *TH*, p. 118 (p. 106).

76. *TH*, p. 119 (pp. 107–108).

77. *PT*, p. 108. This statement appears in the essay, "Wort Gottes und Sprache," one of the two essays in *Perspektiven* which has not been published in English translation. The other is "Verkündigung als Problem der Exegese."

78. *PT*, p. 102.

79. Indeed Langdon Gilkey has characterized Moltmann's theory as a Sabellianism in reverse with the revealed sequence, not Father, then Son, and then Spirit, but Spirit, then Son, with Father coming only in the final consummation. (*Naming the Whirlwind: The Renewal of God-Language* [New York: Bobbs-Merrill, 1969], p. 133, n. 38.)

80. In this connection see Barth's letter of 1924 to his friend, Eduard Thurneysen, where he writes: "A Trinity of *being,* not just an economic Trinity! At all costs the doctrine of the Trinity! If I could get the right key in my hand there, then everything would come out right. . . ." (*Revolutionary Theology in the Making: Barth-Thurneysen Correspondence, 1914–1925,* trans. James D. Smart [Richmond: John Knox Press, 1964], p. 176). Also from another letter in the same year: "I understand the Trinity as *the problem of the inalienable subjectivity of God in his revelation* and I cannot withhold my approval from Athanasius who in general must have been quite a man. The moderns are naturally sad brothers at this point, too: Sabellians and other undesireabilities" (ibid., p. 185).

81. *CG*, p. 240 (p. 227). Moltmann is here appropriating the words of Karl Rahner.

82. Jürgen Moltmann, "The 'Crucified God': God and the Trinity Today," *New Questions on God*, ed. Johannes B. Metz, p. 35.

CHAPTER III

1. *PT*, p. 126. *Sprachereignis* may also be translated "speech-event."

2. See James Robinson's discussion of this point in *The New Hermeneutic*, ed. James M. Robinson and John B. Cobb, Jr., p. 57.

3. *TH*, p. 85 (p. 75). Ebeling, following Luther, also characterizes the "word-event" of the gospel as "promise." But his argument that "what came to expression in Jesus continues to come to expression" in this word-event and that "where word happens rightly, existence is illumined" fails, in Moltmann's judgment, to do justice to the promised future of Jesus which has not yet come to full expression and which thus serves more to contradict than to "illumine" the present state of existence. See Gerhard Ebeling's *Word and Faith*, trans. James W. Leitch (Philadelphia: Fortress Press, 1963), p. 298 and p. 327.

4. See W.D. Davies' lexical reference to Yahweh "swearing" rather than "promising" in *The Gospel and the Land: Early Christianity and Jewish Territorial Doctrine* (Berkeley: University of California Press, 1974), p. 15, n. 1. Claus Westermann has also stressed that *epangelia* is a New Testament and not an Old Testament conception. (*Essays on Old Testament Hermeneutics*, ed. Claus Westermann, p. 131.)

5. *RRF*, p. 211.

6. *TH*, pp. 111–112 (p. 100).

7. *TH*, p. 112 (p. 101).

8. See above, p. 35.

9. *TH*, p. 188 (p. 171).

10. *RRF*, p. 99 (*PT*, p. 140).

11. *TH*, p. 223 (p. 204).

12. *RRF*, p. 215.

13. *RRF*, p. 193. The term "function" itself requires a more precise definition than Moltmann provides.

14. *TH*, pp. 102–106 (pp. 92–95). Zimmerli's essay, "Promise and Fulfillment," is translated in *Essays on Old Testament Hermeneutics*, cited above.

15. "Promise and Fulfillment," *Essays on Old Testament Hermeneutics*, p. 89.

16. *TH*, p. 104 (p. 93), italics mine. Elsewhere Moltmann speaks of this character as "the invariable" in the hermeneutical process. *RRF*, p. 103 (*PT*, pp. 142–143).

17. *TH*, p. 73 (p. 64).

18. *TH*, p. 75 (p. 66).

19. See Georg Picht, *Die Erfahrung der Geschichte* (Frankfurt: Vittorio Klostermann, 1958). This treatise consists of but fifty–four pages, but it is essential in order to recognize the background of some of Moltmann's major conceptions.

20. The explicit references are as follows: *TH*, p. 28 (pp. 23–24); p. 41 (p. 34); p.47, n. 2 (p. 40, n. 16); *HP*, p. 104 (*PT*, p. 152); p. 105 (pp. 153–154); p. 182 (p. 259); *Diskussion über die 'Theologie der Hoffnung*,' p. 218.

21. See Martin Heidegger, *Being and Time*, a translation of *Sein Und Zeit* by John Macquarrie and Edward Robinson (New York: Harper & Row, 1962), "Introduction," pp. 21–64. Picht writes: "If this attempt proves to be successful in penetrating the experience of history, then it is indebted to that experience of thinking by means of which my teacher, Martin Heidegger, opened up our question in a new perspective. That is why the course of this inquiry occurs step by step in a discussion with his way of thinking . . . and I am most deeply indebted to him precisely at those points where in the foreground of my considerations I seem to depart from him." *Die Erfahrung der Geschichte*, pp. 5–6. Although Moltmann provides several critiques of Heidegger— see especially *TH*, pp. 255–261 (pp. 234–239); and *HP*, pp. 72–77 (*PT*, pp. 73–79); pp. 89–91 (pp. 90–92)—he nowhere expresses disagreement with Picht.

22. Georg Picht, *Die Erfahrung der Geschichte*, p. 42.

23. Ibid., p. 45.

24. Ibid., p. 44.

25. *HP*, p. 17 (*PT*, p. 27).

26. Picht, *Die Erfahrung der Geschichte*, p. 48.

27. *RRF*, p. 210.

28. Picht, *Die Erfahrung der Geschichte*, pp. 48, 50.

29. *HP*, p. 183 (*PT*, p. 253).

30. Picht, *Die Erfahrung der Geschichte*, p. 48.

31. *HP*, p. 15 (*PT*, p. 25). Elsewhere, *HP*, p. 198 (*PT*, pp. 254–255), Moltmann cites this exact statement in Picht which he here appropriates, but this time no citation is given. The German texts are as follows:

Picht: "Sie stellt nicht vor, was unabhängig von ihr schon ist, sondern bringt zur Gegenwart, was noch nicht ist."

Moltmann: "Denn die christliche Offenbarung stellt doch nicht etwas vor, was unabhängig von ihr schon da wäre, immer schon anginge oder ewig sei, sondern sie bringt zur Gegenwart, was noch nicht ist, präsentiert Zukunft und ruft Nichtseiendes ins Dasein."

32. Moltmann does not deny the historic nature of human existence. His argument is that such an existential self-understanding must be united with an understanding of the world as history, a "coordination" which is made possible by "the apostolic process of history which God's revelation calls to life in promise," *TH*, p. 86 (p. 76).

33. *TH*, p. 243 (p. 222).

34. *TH*, p. 270 (p. 248).

35. *TH*, p. 203 (p. 184).

36. *TH*, pp. 163–164 (p. 147).

37. *TH*, p. 225 (p. 205).

38. *RRF*, p. 28.

39. *RRF*, p. 32. Barth also refers to "the negation of the negative." See his *Epistle to the Romans*, pp. 142 and 182, for example.

40. *TH*, p. 131 (p. 118).

41. Jürgen Moltmann, *Diskussion über die 'Theologie der Hoffnung,'* p. 206.

42. For an examination of the sorts of decisions involved in determining such congruence see David H. Kelsey, *The Uses of Scripture in Recent Theology*, esp. pp. 196–197.

43. A similar point has been made by Juan Luis Segundo, S.J. from the perspective of Latin American liberation theologies. He mentions with apparently some surprise that some Americans who speak of liberation theology "question the necessity of returning to the sources or fonts of *Christian* revelation." He writes: "One can certainly move on to a new

theology or a different tradition of 'revelation.' What seems odd to me is that any such new theology would continue to call itself 'Christian,' as they often do.'' *The Liberation of Theology*, trans. John Drury (Maryknoll, N.Y.: Orbis Books, 1976), pp. 37–38.

44. It is true, however, that the Wisdom literature of the Old Testament is scarcely mentioned in Moltmann's proposals, and those parts of the New Testament which are more amenable to the notion of a "realized eschatology" are generally left unexamined. Moltmann's thesis is not a denial that such "epiphanic" elements are there, but the contention that they occur within a more all embracing boundary of apocalyptic expectation.

45. In this connection one should note the debate between D. Friedrich Baumgärtel and Claus Westermann on the question of promise as an Old Testament conception. Baumgärtel's position, in brief, is that there is a "basic promise" (*Grundverheissung*) expressed in Yahweh's pledge of himself to his people: "I am the Lord your God." This is the link between Old Testament faith as expectation and New Testament faith in the realization which comes in Jesus Christ. Westermann's criticism is that the notion of a "basic promise" is an abstraction which has no validity with respect to the Old Testament itself. Baumgärtel, in Westermann's view, has imposed a Lutheran reading of the New Testament *epangelia* upon the Old Testament, where it does not fit. Westermann's own analysis postulates not one but three basic forms of promise: 1) a pledge of salvation, 2) a prediction of coming events, and 3) a portrayal of a universal future. See D. Friedrich Baumgärtel, *Verheissung: Zur Frage des evangelischen Verständnisses des Alten Testaments* (Gutersloh: C. Bertelsmann Verlag, 1952); also, "The Hermeneutical Problem of the Old Testament," *Essays on Old Testament Hermeneutics,* ed. Claus Westermann, pp. 134–159. Westermann's critique, "Remarks on the Theses of Bultmann and Baumgärtel," appears in this same volume of essays, pp. 122–133. Westermann's own view of promise appears in "The Way of the Promise through the Old Testament," *The Old Testament and Christian Faith,* ed. Bernhard W. Anderson (New York: Harper & Row, 1963), pp. 200–223.

46. *HP,* p. 86 (*PT,* p. 88).

47. In reviewing the trends in biblical theology since the Second

World War, Brevard S. Childs has written: "Although there was the widest possible agreement among the Biblical theologians in regard to revelation in history, there was an equally wide spectrum of differing interpretations respecting the nature of history, revelation, and their relationship." *Biblical Theology in Crisis* (Philadelphia: Westminster Press, 1970) p. 44.

48. See especially Barth's discussion of "The Nature of the Word of God," *Church Dogmatics,* vol. 1, pt. 1, par. 5. Barth's word for "language" here is *Rede* rather than *Sprache*.

49. Ibid., p. 163.

50. Ibid., p. 150. The context here clearly suggests an affirmation of "ordinary meaning."

51. Ibid., p. 151.

52. Ibid., p. 57. For a criticism of Barth on this point see Donald Evans, "Barth on Talk About God," *CJT* 16, nos. 3 and 4 (1970), pp. 175–192. Evans writes, "If human words as such provide nothing towards knowledge of God, this implies sheer equivocity between their meaning as applied to men and their meaning as applied to God; yet Barth rejects equivocity, for God has made knowledge of God possible, using human words" p. 190.

53. Ibid., pp. 189–190.

54. Ibid., p. 154.

55. Ibid., p. 153.

56. See above, p. 53.

57. Karl Barth, *Church Dogmatics, The Doctrine of Creation*, vol. 3, pt. 2, "The Phenomena of the Human," trans. Harold Knight, G.W. Bromiley, J. K. S. Reid, R. H. Fuller (Edinburgh: T. & T. Clark, 1960), pp. 71–132.

58. Dallas High has criticized this Barthian assumption, not with respect to revelatory language, but with a concern to point out the "personal backing" which characterizes belief utterances. *Language, Persons and Belief* (New York: Oxford University Press, 1967), pp. 191–193. According to Barth, Anselm's claim that genuine rationality in thought mirrors a rationality in being is not to be considered primarily as an expression of Platonic Realism but as an affirmation of how knowledge of God is given in revelation. Barth, in analysing the *Proslogium*, thus minimizes the "Neo-Platonic technique of the ex-

position" and presents Anslem's conviction that the *noetic* corresponds to the *ontic* and is determined by it as "a confidence based on faith and faith alone." *Anselm: Fides Quaerens Intellectum: Anselm's Proof of the Existence of God in the Context of his Theological Scheme*, trans. Ian W. Robertson (London: SCM Press, 1960), p. 58 and p. 52.

59. Karl Barth, *Church Dogmatics*, vol. 1, pt. 2, p. 464.

60. *TH*, pp. 76–84 (pp. 67–74). "Direct" in this instance does not mean "immediate" in the sense of non-mediated. From a philosophical point of view a "direct" and an "immediate" experience of God are distinguished by John Smith in *Reason and God* (New Haven: Yale University Press, 1961), pp. 181–182.

61. *Theology As History*, vol. 3, *New Frontiers in Theology*, ed. James M. Robinson and John B. Cobb, Jr., pp. 254–255, n. 61.

62. *TH*, p.88 (p.78).

63. Note again the fourth of the seven marks of a promise adapted from Zimmerli as referred to above, p. 53.

64. *HP*, p. 17 (*PT*, p. 27).

65. *HP*, p. 184 (*PT*, p. 256).

66. See above, p. 14.

67. Jürgen Moltmann, "Theology As Eschatology," *The Future of Hope*, p. 19.

68. *RRF*, p. 14. Italics mine.

69. See James Barr, *Semantiçs of Biblical Language* (London: Oxford University Press, 1961). Of this text Brevard Childs writes, "Seldom has one book brought down so much superstructure with such effectiveness." (*Biblical Theology in Crisis*, p. 72.)

70. In a critical review of Moltmann's *Theology of Hope* Hans Frei writes: "It does not seem that it is divinely ordained that we must swap an empiricist for an historicist, dialectical or ideological outlook before we can do theology. If it is, then heaven (literally!) help the theologian on the current Anglo-American scene." *USQR* 23, no. 3 (Spring 1968), p. 271.

71. H.A. Prichard, "The Obligation to Keep a Promise" (c. 1940), published in *Moral Obligation* (Oxford: Clarendon Press, 1949), p. 170.

72. Ibid., p. 179.

73. For a discussion of the background of Austin's thought and for

criticism of his views, see the essays in *Symposium on J.L. Austin,* ed. K.T. Fann (New York: Humanities Press, 1969).

74. See J.L. Austin, "Performative Utterances" (1956), *Philosophical Papers* (Oxford: Clarendon Press, 1961), pp. 220–239.

75. J.L. Austin, "Other Minds," *Philosophical Papers,* p. 71.

76. J.L. Austin, "Performative Utterances," *Philosophical Papers,* p. 222.

77. Ibid., p. 223.

78. Ibid., p. 228.

79. Ibid., p. 233.

80. Ibid., p. 238.

81. Edited by J.O. Urmson and published posthumously as *How to Do Things With Words* (Cambridge: Harvard University Press, 1962).

82. See *How to Do Things With Words,* pp. 98–119, for what follows.

83. Ibid., p. 98.

84. Ibid., pp. 150–163.

85. Ibid., pp. 150–151.

86. Ibid., p. 162.

87. Donald Evans, *The Logic of Self-Involvement: A Philosophical Study of Everyday Language with Special Reference to the Christian Use of Language About God as Creator* (London: SCM Press, 1963).

88. Ibid., p. 164.

89. Ibid., p. 165.

90. Ibid., p. 158.

91. On this latter point Evans writes: "The provision of a logic for theology need not involve the dictation of particular answers to particular theological questions. Indeed, a logic may provide a framework within which theologians can *dis*agree intelligibly. . . . On the other hand, a new logic may very well be in tension with earlier theologies insofar as these are bound up with earlier logics." (Ibid., p. 21.)

92. Ibid., 124ff. Evans' choice of the term "onlook" is not an altogether satisfactory one in that it is used to suggest the very opposite stance to that of an uninvolved onlooker in the sense of a mere spectator.

93. Ibid., p. 160.

94. Ibid., p. 114. In Evans' linguistic classification Behabitives as

well as Commissives, among the five classes of performatives designated by Austin, display a self-involving logic, as does language which is "expressive" of the speaker's feeling though it may not qualify as either of these performatives in the strict sense of the word.

95. John Searle, *Speech Acts: An Essay in the Philosophy of Language* (Cambridge: Cambridge University Press, 1970).

96. Ibid., pp. 57–64. I have slightly modified some of the technical shorthand of Searle's own expression here.

97. Ibid., p. 61.

98. Ibid., pp. 63–64.

99. Ibid.

100. Ibid., p. 125.

101. Ibid., p. 146. Searle contends that the fallacy of "meaning as use" is responsible for several major dilemmas in contemporary philosophy.

102. Ibid., p. 198.

103. Here I refer mainly to the *semantical* "facts" which Austin, Evans, and Searle describe. There is in addition the *syntactical* question of "linguistic competence" and "generative grammar" raised by Noam Chomsky. See, for example, Chomsky's *Aspects of the Theory of Syntax* (Cambridge: M.I.T. Press, 1965), pp. 3–62, and *Language and Mind* (New York: Harcourt, Brace and World, 1968). Whatever the eventual outcome of linguistic research, it is clear that the enterprise cannot be disregarded as irrelevant by any theology of the Word which refuses to divorce itself from human speech.

104. See above, p. 44.

105. Dietrich Bonhoeffer mistakenly tries to separate the "how" from the "who" questions in *Christ the Center,* trans. John Bowden (New York: Harper & Row, 1966), p. 33: "The Christological question is fundamentally an ontological question. Its aim is to work out the ontological structure of the 'Who?' without coming to grief on the Scylla of the question 'How?' (*Wie-Frage*) or the Charybdis of the question of the 'fact' of revelation (*Dass-Frage*)." This separation cannot be maintained in practice as Bonhoeffer's own discussion plainly demonstrates.

106. Pannenberg's concern to move beyond both direct referentiality and the problems posed by indirect inferentiality in accounting for the

meaning of revelation is worth noting here. "Knowledge of the history of Jesus as an anticipation of the future general definition of humanity . . . is a knowledge of the meaning of this history as promise, and thus leads to trust in 'the God who raised Jesus from the dead'. . . . The clearer the knowledge of this unique character of the history of Jesus is, the more clearly it points beyond its own form as theoretical knowledge into faith. For thus it will be more clearly recognized that the only ultimately appropriate behavior toward this history is not mere cognizance but trust in the God proclaimed by Jesus." (*Theology As History*, pp. 267–268.) The linguistic analyses of what Pannenberg calls "this unique character" of promise enable us to see even on logical grounds why revelatory knowledge must be said to involve "not mere cognizance but trust."

107. In a response to Searle, R.M. Hare has issued the following caution. "Here there is a trap to be avoided. Some occurrences of the verb 'promise' which are not themselves performances of the speech act of promising are to be explained as reports or predictions or in general statements that such an act has been or is being or will be performed." "Meaning and Speech Acts," *PhRev* (January, 1970), p. 8.

108. *TH*, p. 179 (p. 162).

109. See above p. 66.

110. In this connection it is interesting to note Pannenberg's rejoinder to a criticism of Sauter that the term "prolepsis" as Pannenberg uses it is a teleological rather than a suitably eschatological construct. "The real difference between us may lie elsewhere . . . in the question whether the eschatological future so understood has to be conceived in pure opposition to the logic of the phenomena. . . . It may be that the motivation for the antithetical assertions in Moltmann as in Sauter is to be sought in the tendency to oppose the 'promise' to the whole natural situation of man. But this supernaturalism cannot be carried through without depriving the promise itself of its meaning as promise. For a future that is *only* opposed to the presently existing world cannot be a 'promise' for it, but can only mean threat and destruction. Sauter has himself observed that the idea of promise implies a positive relationship to the presently existing reality to which the promise applies. . . . If this insight is taken seriously, then the dualism cannot be maintained between eschatological future (and

promise) on the one hand, and the presently existing world of 'phenomena' on the other." (*Theology As History,* p. 262.) The "dualism" which Pannenberg alleges here would more properly be addressed to Barth's position than to Moltmann's if it were recognized that the form of promise is precisely, for Moltmann, the one presently existing reality which is not opposed to the eschatological future. It is only from the starting point of a logic of promise that what Pannenberg calls "a logic of presently existing phenomena" can be eschatologically understood. Otherwise, as Moltmann rightly sees, *continuity* in the dynamics of revelation becomes misconceived as the congruence of revelation with world reality as it presently exists.

111. Jerome Schneewind, to whom Searle refers on this point, argues that "the promisor must have good reason to believe that the promisee wants the promised act to be done, if the words spoken by the promisor are to serve to put him under an obligation." "A Note on Promising," *Philosophical Studies* 17, no. 3 (April, 1966), p. 34. Such reasoning is clearly not applicable to any biblical understanding of God whose revelation is at once seen as the world's judgment and its hope.

112. John Searle, *Speech Acts,* p. 58, italics mine.

113. *HP,* p. 138 (*PT,* p. 220).

CHAPTER IV

1. See "Toward the Next Step in the Dialogue," *The Future of Hope,* p. 156.

2. John E. Smith, *Experience and God* (New York: Oxford University Press, 1968), p. 21.

3. Ibid., p. 49.

4. Jürgen Moltmann, *HP,* pp. 15–16 (*PT,* pp. 25–26).

5. *TH,* p. 18 (p. 13).

6. "The Problem of Continuity," *The Future of Hope,* pp. 78–79.

7. "The Universal and Immediate Presence of God," ibid., p. 100. See also Gilkey's essay, "The Contribution of Culture to the Reign of God," in *The Future as the Presence of Shared Hope,* ed. Maryellen Muckenhirn (New York: Sheed and Ward, 1968), pp. 34–58, and the more recent references to Moltmann in the same connection in *Reaping The Whirlwind: A Christian Interpretation of History* (New York: Seabury Press, 1976), esp. pp. 233–236.

8. "Secularism, Responsible Belief, and the 'Theology of Hope'," ibid., p. 144.

9. James Gustafson, "The Conditions for Hope: Reflections on Human Experience," *Continuum* 7, no. 4 (Winter, 1970), p. 541.

10. Moltmann generally uses the word *Erfahrung* rather than *Erlebnis,* but the distinction is not emphasized in his argument.

11. *TH,* p. 18 (pp. 13–14).

12. *TH,* p. 17 (p. 13).

13. Jürgen Moltmann, *Diskussion über die 'Theologie der Hoffnung,'* p. 212.

14. *RRF,* p. 118.

15. *TH,* p. 89 (p. 79).

16. *RRF,* p. 210. Italics mine.

17. *TH,* p. 191 (p. 174). Italics mine.

18. *RRF,* p. 210. Italics mine.

19. *RRF,* pp. 28–29. Italics mine.

20. *HP,* pp. 15–17 (*PT,* pp. 25–26). Italics mine.

21. Rom. 8:24b.

22. Other ideas pertaining to *experience* which one might expect to find here, such as *pathos* and *aisthesis* (the latter mentioned only once, on p. 32), are not considered. Cf. F.E. Peters, *Greek Philosophical Terms: A Historical Lexicon* (New York: New York University Press, 1967), pp. 9–15, 152–155. Also, Picht does not distinguish significant points of difference among the Greeks.

23. Georg Picht, *Die Erfahrung der Geschichte*, p. 46.

24. Ibid., p. 13.

25. Ibid., p. 15. Picht quotes the definition of "experience" given by the physicist and philosopher C.F. von Weizsäcker: "the perception (*Erkenntnis*) of a universal fact (*eines allgemeinen Sachverhalts*) on the basis of observation (*Wahrnehmungen*)." It is this definition he has in mind when he refers to "the objective science of modern times."

26. Ibid., p. 16.

27. Ibid., p. 24.

28. Ibid., p. 22.

29. Ibid., p. 26.

30. Loc. cit.

31. *TH,* p. 47 (p. 40).

32. *TH*, p. 41 (pp. 34–35).

33. Part of the problem with appeals to "experience" in some American empirical theologies is that the boundaries of what counts as "experience" are drawn so broadly and vaguely that the appeal is rendered meaningless. Schubert Ogden refers to "a whole range of observings, encounterings, and undergoings, from perceiving the world through our senses to becoming aware of the beautiful and of the claim of the good." "Present Prospects for Empirical Theology," *The Future of Empirical Theology*, ed. Bernard E. Meland (Chicago: University of Chicago Press, 1969), pp. 65–66. Daniel Day Williams writes, "First, by experience I mean the felt, bodily, psycho-social, organic action of human beings in history. Experience includes the sense data, but it is not limited to them." "Suffering and Being in Empirical Theology," *The Future of Empirical Theology*, p. 176. John E. Smith defines "experience" as "a great mass of contents resulting from the interplay between the self and the world in which it lives." *Reason and God* (New Haven: Yale University Press, 1961), p. 174. Since the word is often stretched to encompass both the conscious and the unconscious, or the animate and the inanimate—as in the assertion that "experience" is the interaction of any organism with its environment—as an appeal in theology it is in danger of becoming as obscurantist as the forms of supernaturalism which it seeks to replace.

34. For Alfred North Whitehead's influential description of experience as "causal efficacy" and "presentational immediacy" in the "mixed mode of perception . . . named 'symbolic reference' " see chap. 8, "Symbolic Reference," in *Process and Reality: An Essay in Cosmology* (New York: Harper Torchbooks, 1960), pp. 255–279. Note also, in this connection, David Tracy's statement that "the present need becomes that of finding symbolic language which can allow the disclosure of the Christian God to 'happen' for the present actual situation." *Blessed Rage for Order: The New Pluralism in Theology* (New York: Seabury Press, 1975), p. 189.

35. *TH*, p. 98 (p. 109).

36. *TH*, p. 195 (p. 177).

37. *TH*, p. 262 (p. 240).

38. *TH*, p. 230 (p. 210).

39. *TH*, p. 232 (p. 212).

40. *RRF*, p. xiii.

41. *RRF*, p. 195.

42. *HP*, p. 84 (*PT*, p. 85).

43. *CG*, p. 114 (p. 107).

44. *TH*, pp. 238ff. (pp. 218ff.).

45. *TH*, p. 180 (p. 163).

46. *HP*, p. 89 (*PT*, pp. 90–91).

47. *TH*, p. 284 (pp. 261–262).

48. *HP*, p. 57 (*PT*, p. 58).

49. *TH*, p. 81 (p. 72).

50. *TH*, pp. 83–84 (p. 74). This comment is made in criticism of Pannenberg's discussion in *Revelation As History*.

51. *TH*, pp. 241–245 (pp. 220–224).

52. *TH*, p. 243 (p. 222).

53. *TH*, p. 245 (p. 224).

54. *TH*, p. 197 (p. 179).

55. *TH*, p. 181 (pp. 163–164).

56. *TH*, p. 258 (p. 237).

57. *RRF*, pp. 102–103 (*PT*, pp. 142–143).

58. *TH*, p. 203 (p. 184). It is interesting to see that in his more recent work on ecclesiology Moltmann writes, ''Through the messianic history of Christ a promise and a tendency (*Tendenz*) has been implanted in the church . . .'' *The Church in the Power of the Spirit: A Contribution to Messianic Ecclesiology*, trans. Margaret Kohl (New York: Harper & Row, 1977), p. 24 (p. 38). Hereafter referred to as *CS*. The original text is *Kirche in der Kraft des Geistes* (Munich: Chr. Kaiser Verlag, 1975).

59. In this connection the critical response to Moltmann of two American theologians is instructive. James Robinson expresses the hope that ''in his trajectory from Barth to Bloch'' Moltmann will seek further ''to spell out the implications of performatory language as doing something that affects the future.'' ''The Hermeneutic of Hope,'' *Continuum* 7, no. 4 (Winter, 1970), pp. 528–529. Hans Frei writes, ''It is a vexing problem to know if the crucifixion and resurrection finally are, in the logic of Moltmann's argument, crucial instances of the dialectical process or the actual determination of its rationale.'' ''Review of *Theology of Hope*,'' *USQR* 23, no. 3 (Spring, 1968), p.

269. Whereas Robinson urges that attention be given to the philosophy of language of the later Heidegger, and Frei suggests that one possible solution may be available in the metaphysics of process philosophy, I am interested rather in determining the dogmatic conclusions which can be theoretically accounted for on the basis of an analysis of promise and narrative in ordinary discourse.

60. *TH,* p. 188 (p. 170).

61. *HP,* pp. 75–76 (*PT,* p. 77).

62. W.B. Gallie, *Philosophy and the Historical Understanding* (New York: Schocken Books, 1964 and 1968); Arthur C. Danto, *Analytical Philosophy of History* (Cambridge: At the University Press, 1965). A third text dealing with historical narration often mentioned in connection with these is Morton White's *Foundations of Historical Knowledge* (New York: Harper & Row, 1965). A number of critical reviews of these works have appeared in the journal *History and Theory* (Mouton, 1960–   ).

63. W.B. Gallie, *Philosophy and the Historical Understanding,* p. 1.

64. Ibid., p. 23.

65. Ibid., p. 52.

66. The issue of "explanations" as it relates to narrative is a complex and much debated one in the recent critical philosophy of history. For a comparison and critique of the views of Gallie, Danto, and White on this point see Louis O. Mink, "Philosophical Analysis and Historical Understanding," *Review of Metaphysics* 21 (1968), pp. 667–698. For a discussion of the theological importance of developing the "import" of narration and not simply assuming that "telling the story is the whole thing" see Julian N. Hartt, "Story As the Art of Historical Truth," chap. 8 in *Theological Method and Imagination* (New York: Seabury Press, 1977), pp. 219–254.

67. W.B. Gallie, *Philosophy and the Historical Understanding,* p. 107. Gallie's words could serve as an apt description of the purpose of "explanations" in Christian theology as well. In this connection see Hans Frei's account of how the meaning of Scripture came to be explained in ways other than by appeal to its form as "realistic narrative" in eighteenth and nineteenth century hermeneutics: *The Eclipse of Biblical Narrative* (New Haven: Yale University Press, 1974).

68. Arthur Danto, *Analytical Philosophy of History,* p. 11.

69. Ibid., p. 143.

70. Ibid., p. 111.

71. Ibid., p. 9. On this point see Karl Löwith, *Meaning in History* (Chicago: University of Chicago Press, 1949), whom Danto also cites, and J.L. Talmon, *Political Messianism: The Romantic Phase* (London: Secker and Warburg, 1960). Talmon writes, "It is of course no accident that every Messianic thinker" (he is speaking in a secular political sense) "sooner or later had to come to grips with religion," p. 208.

72. W.B. Gallie, *Philosophy and the Historical Understanding*, pp. 64–65.

73. Ibid., p. 28. Here it is worth noting that Gallie has been criticized for not recognizing that his thesis, viz., that events are connected in terms of their "mutual orientation toward the promised end," applies primarily if one is "following" a narrative which is not complete, or which, if complete, one has not followed to the conclusion previously. Louis Mink suggests that at least with respect to the historian's craft, the case is usually that one *has* followed a story many times previously to its end and that the decisive action in historical understanding is more exactly one of "having followed" rather than, as Gallie puts it, one of "following." See "History and Fiction as Modes of Comprehension," *New Literary History* 1 (Spring, 1970), pp. 541–558. Thus one must admit that, contrary to Gallie, "time is not of the essence of narratives," p. 555. Mink offers his own corrective: "But in the configurational comprehension of a story which one *has followed*, the end is connected with the promise of the beginning as well as the beginning with the promise of the end, and the necessity of the backward references cancels out, so to speak, the contingency of the forward references. To comprehend temporal succession means to think of it in both directions at once, and then time is no longer the river which bears us along but the river in aerial view, upstream and downstream seen in a single survey," pp. 554–555. While this analysis may apply to fiction, in which the author controls events, or to restricted instances in historical research, the theological question remains to be asked if a "historical" narrative can ever be said to be as *finally* concluded as Mink implies. Perhaps the word "promise" here should be taken in more than a vaguely rhetorical sense!

74. W.B. Gallie, *Philosophy and the Historical Understanding*, p. 31.

75. Arthur Danto, *Analytical Philosophy of History*, p. 143.

76. Ibid., p. 151.

77. Ibid., p. 183.

78. Ibid., p. 26.

79. Ibid., p. 142.

80. Ibid., p. 182.

81. Ibid., p. 70. Danto develops this critique in considerable detail by taking up the logical problems posed by the classical issues of historical foreknowledge, human freedom and determinism, and future and past contingencies, which have occupied metaphysicians since the time of Aristotle.

82. Not all critical philosophers of history would place as much emphasis upon this factor of the future as do Gallie and Danto. See, for example, Maurice Mandelbaum's criticism in "A Note on History as Narrative," *History and Theory,* vol. 6, no. 3 (1967), pp. 413–419. Mandelbaum writes, "The relationship which I therefore take to be fundamental in historiography is . . . a relationship of part to whole, not a relationship of antecedent to consequent," pp. 417–418. This debate is taken up by Richard G. Ely, Rolf Gruner, and William H. Dray in "Mandelbaum on Historical Narrative: A Discussion," *History and Theory,* vol. 8, no. 2 (1969), pp. 275–294.

83. I shall quote from Gallie's account here. For references see R.G. Collingwood, *The Idea of History* (New York: Oxford University Press, 1946), pp. 246–247.

84. W.B. Gallie, *Philosophy and the Historical Understanding*, pp. 56–57.

85. Ibid., p. 59.

86. Ibid., p. 61.

87. Ibid., p. 62.

88. Ibid., p. 63.

89. Ibid., p. 124.

90. Arthur Danto, *Analytical Philosophy of History,* p. 25.

91. Ibid., p. 115.

92. Ibid., p. 127.

93. For an example of a contrary view that asserts that there is no "fundamental scheme of intelligibility peculiar to the narrative form itself," see Robert Stover, *The Nature of Historical Thinking* (Chapel Hill: University of North Carolina Press, 1967), p. 70.

94. Of relevant interest in this matter is the following statement by Hans Frei: "Historical accounting, by almost universal modern consent, involves that the narrative satisfactorily rendering a sequence believed to have taken place must consist of events, and reasons for their occurrence, whose connections may be rendered without recourse to supernatural agency. By contrast in the biblical stories, of course, nonmiraculous and miraculous accounts and explanations are constantly intermingled. But in accordance with our definition, even the miraculous accounts are realistic or history-like (but not therefore historical and in that sense factually true) if they do not in effect symbolize something else instead of the action portrayed. That is to say, even such miraculous accounts are history-like or realistic if the depicted action is indispensable to the rendering of a particular character, divine or human, or a particular story." (*The Eclipse of Biblical Narrative*, p. 14.) Can we say that accounts which are "not historical and in that sense factually true" are *ever* (never?) "indispensable" to rendering a character or occurrence *historical*?

95. This accounts in part for the general complaint of some of the more empirically oriented American theologians that Moltmann's view of promise is "too abstract." To the degree that this is so, the reason is to be found, I think, in Moltmann's failure to emphasize the inseparability of "hope-sentences" from "descriptive-sentences" in revelatory language and not in his unwillingness to subscribe to the notion that this language must gain its meaning and truth by corresponding to present experience, as these critics are wont to claim. Yet Moltmann's own too facile willingness to suggest in some places (though not in all) that such meaning and truth are gained by the promise of God merely (abstractly!) negating present experience is also inadequate. Our examination of these issues has attempted to show that the matter is more complex than this.

96. For this reason Moltmann has expressed most interest in those American theologies which address the problem of liberation. See, for example, to cite only one title from the writings of each of three theologians with whom Moltmann has indicated a solidarity, James Cone, *A Black Theology of Liberation* (New York: J.B. Lippincott, 1970); Frederick Herzog, *Liberation Theology* (New York: Seabury Press, 1972); Letty Russell, *Human Liberation in a Feminist Per-*

spective—A Theology (Philadelphia: Westminster Press, 1974). The importance of "story" in a self-involving and world-transforming theological politics is elucidated by Paul Lehmann in *The Transfiguration of Politics* (New York: Harper & Row, 1975). Lehmann writes: "Revolutionary aspiration, struggle, and action are nourished by and generate a rhetoric of promises, goals, and directions. The rhetoric, in turn, feeds upon a saving story. And the power of the story to 'save' is drawn from the appropriateness of the metaphorical indication of the correspondence between the biblical and the human meaning of politics," p. 236. It is precisely the influence of such a "story," Lehmann argues, which serves to prohibit Christian theology from taking its leave of history, or, as he puts it, of seeking "a flight from politics . . . into another kind of world altogether than the world in which revolutions happen" (p. 340, n. 15).

97. This observation runs counter to a generation of existentialist theological thought which has taken Tillich's assertion of the "symbolic" character of revelatory knowledge as axiomatic. "The use of finite materials in their ordinary sense for the knowledge of revelation destroys the meaning of revelation and deprives God of his divinity." Paul Tillich, *Systematic Theology*, vol. 1 (Chicago: University of Chicago Press, 1951), p. 131. To say, however, that the form of promise and the form of narrative are somehow "symbolic" and must not be understood in their "ordinary sense" when they appear in revelatory language would be unwarranted exegetically and incomprehensible logically.

98. It is curious that after a thorough insistence upon a recognition of the relation of historical judgments to Christian belief Van Harvey propounds the thesis that faith, as a "confidence in the nature of being itself" which "must have some basis in one's present experience," sees in Jesus Christ a "perspective image" for "relating one to present reality." *The Historian and the Believer* (New York: Macmillan, 1966), p. 283. The idea of "promissory narration," I submit, is more consonant with historical understanding than is "perspective image." The question of the kind of relation one has to present reality is crucial. Harvey recognizes possible problems with his position when he writes, "The basic objection to some such model as this, I am aware, is that it reduces Jesus to a symbol of some timeless truth" (p. 285).

99. For a brief introduction to some of the questions which must be faced in this connection see Johann Baptist Metz, "A Short Apology of Narrative," *The Crisis of Religious Language,* ed. Johann Baptist Metz and Jean-Pierre Jossua, *Concilium,* no. 85 (New York: Herder and Herder, 1973), pp. 84–96. Metz's failure, however, to take into consideration any of the linguistic examinations which have been made of narration in contemporary analytical philosophy severely limits the range of his reflections.

CHAPTER V

1. *RRF,* p. 216.
2. "Theology as Eschatology," *The Future of Hope,* p. 9.
3. *HP,* p. 25 (*PT,* p. 34).
4. *TH,* p. 223 (p. 203).
5. It is instructive to note in this connection Reginald Fuller's remarks concerning "the necessity of ontology" in *The Foundations of New Testament Christology* (New York: Charles Scribner's Sons, 1965), pp. 247–259. "The NT scholar," Fuller writes, "cannot suggest to the contemporary systematic theologian that he by-pass the whole ontological problem in favour of a purely functional Christology. But he must insist that the functional affirmations of the earliest Jewish Christology inevitably lead to the ontic affirmations of the gentile mission, and that these in turn raise pressing ontological questions" (p. 256).
6. *CG,* p. 5 (p. 10).
7. *CS,* pp. 29–30 (p. 45).
8. *CG,* p. 113 (pp. 106–107).
9. *TH,* p. 137 (p. 124).
10. "Theology as Eschatology," *The Future of Hope,* p. 16.
11. See "Theology as Eschatology," in *The Future of Hope,* pp. 1–50, and esp. pp. 9–16. In referring to "God as Future" Moltmann explains, "Here I appropriate a certain harmony of ideas expressed by J.B. Metz, W. Pannenberg, and myself in the Festschrift, *Ernst Bloch zu ehren* (1965)," (n. 11, p. 9). Some of the same points are made in *RRF,* pp. 208–210.
12. Ernst Bloch, *Atheism in Christianity,* p. 265.
13. "Theology As Eschatology," *The Future of Hope,* p. 10.

14. Ibid., p. 11.

15. Ibid., p. 14.

16. *RRF*, p. 61.

17. *HP*, p. *181* (*PT*, pp. 253–254).

18. "Theology As Eschatology," *The Future of Hope*, pp. 11–12.

19. Ibid., p. 12.

20. Ibid., p. 13.

21. The formative notion is that of "imminent arrival" (*bevorstehende Ankunft*). *TH*, p. 227 (p. 207).

22. *TH*, p. 114 (pp. 102–103).

23. *HP*, p. 51 (*PT*, p. 55).

24. *CG*, p. 247 (pp. 233–234).

25. *CG*, p. 249 (pp 235–236).

26. According to biblical faith it is the story of *God's* commitment and constancy, and not of their own, which identifies human beings as persons. This prevents us from defining "person" in terms of some particular human capacity.

27. I would apply the same point also to those theologies which attempt to provide backing for the position that God is a person, or personal, by appealing to self-authenticating I-Thou encounters. See, for example, Ronald Hepburn's critique of this position in *Christianity and Paradox* (London: C.A. Watts & Co., 1958), pp. 24–59. For a discussion from the perspective of Whiteheadean process theologies of whether or not God should be described metaphysically as an "actual entity" or a "living person" see William A. Christian, *An Interpretation of Whitehead's Metaphysics* (New Haven: Yale University Press, 1959), pp. 409–411 and John B. Cobb, Jr., *A Christian Natural Theology* (Philadelphia: Westminster Press, 1965), pp. 71–79 and 188–192.

28. *HP*, p. 20 (*PT*, p. 29).

29. Moltmann writes: "Omega is more than Alpha. . . . The original creation was created out of the will of God. But in its future God will dwell in it with his essence. This is to say that the new creation corresponds to the essence of God and is illuminated and transfigured by God's earthly presence." *RRF*, p. 36.

30. See *TH*, pp. 154f. (pp. 140f.). *CG* represents a continuation and extension of this theme, not a change in direction.

31. *CG*, p. 190 (p. 177).

32. *CG*, p. 193 (p. 180). *"Stasis"* here suggests an "over-againstness" within the being of God.

33. For a further discussion of this point see Emil L. Fackenheim, *The Religious Dimension in Hegel's Thought* (Bloomington: Indiana University Press, 1967). "Hegel's Spirit—which is free internal self-development—*includes* Matter, which is unfree externality, brute givenness, and chance" (p. 19). "Spirit has the power of what he calls overreaching (*übergreifen*)" (p. 20), "perhaps Hegel's most important term" (p. 98). "Christian life includes the agony of Good Friday, even though the bliss of Easter overreaches it"(p. 149).

34. *TH*, pp. 171–172 (p. 155).

35. *CG*, p. 207 (p. 192).

36. *CG*, p. 246 (p. 233).

37. *CG*, p. 249 (p. 235).

38. *HP*, p. 15 (*PT*, p. 24).

39. *CG*, p. 203 (p. 188).

40. *RRF*, p. 210.

41. *CG*, pp. 255–256 (p. 242). It is surprising to find Moltmann quoting uncritically in approval Whitehead's description of the Galilean spirit of tender love as one which "finds purpose in the present immediacy of a kingdom not of this world" and which "does not look to the future; for it finds its own reward in the immediate present" p. 250 (p. 237).

42. *CG*, p. 255 (p. 242).

43. *CG*, p. 277 (p. 266).

44. *CG*, p. 246 (pp. 232–233).

45. *CG*, p. 245 (p. 232).

46. *CG*, p. 337 (p. 314).

47. *CG*, p. 246 (p. 232).

48. See above, p. 46.

49. Karl Barth, *The Humanity of God*, trans. John Newton Thomas (Richmond: John Knox Press, 1960), p. 50.

50. This is more clearly the case in *The Crucified God* where Moltmann speaks of overcoming "the dichotomy" between the immanent and the economic Trinity. *CG*, p. 245 (p. 232). In his later work, *The Church in the Power of the Spirit*, Moltmann's position

comes closer to Barth's: "As God appears in history as the sending Father and the sent Son, so he must earlier have been in himself. The relation of the one who sends to the one sent as it appears in the history of Jesus thus includes in itself an order of origin within the Trinity, and must be understood as that order's historical correspondence. . . . The *missio ad extra* reveals the *missio ad intra*. The *missio ad intra* is the foundation for the *missio ad extra.*" CS, p. 54 (p. 70). There is a Trinity in origin (*Ursprung*) distinguishable from the Trinity of mission (*Sendung*). This Trinity of origin is not, as in Barth's view of the immanent Trinity, a "closed circle." The technical difference in the two positions here is that for Barth the divine decision of election which institutes God's relation to an "other" than himself, i.e., to creation, is not a decision which *constitutes* the triunity of God's being, though it flows from it. For Moltmann the decision of election is constitutive of the Trinity in its very *Ursprung*. If this is a correct reading, it would be consistent with the notion that God's own being is intrinsically promissory, though Moltmann in this text does not spell out further his discussion of *promissio* in relation to the *missio ad intra* and *ad extra*.

51. *HP*, p. 23 (*PT*, p. 32).

52. *RRF*, p. 61.

53. For a critique of attempts to understand God's being as triune by appealing to the form of revelation see Cyril C. Richardson, *The Doctrine of the Trinity* (New York: Abingdon Press, 1958), pp. 118–132. The Sabellian issue, Richardson argues, is not only that the persons of the Godhead are regarded merely as "transitory and successive phases of revelation" but that "the fundamental paradox of God's absolute and related character" and "the necessary threeness of these distinctions" cannot be explained in revelational terms. "It is not in the manner or manners in which God is revealed that the primary problem lies. Rather it is to be seen in the fact that beside his revealed and related nature, there stands his hiddenness and beyondness" (pp. 125–126). For Moltmann, however, it is precisely that "manner" in which God is revealed that prohibits theology from conceiving of a "hiddenness and beyondness" beside the "revealed and related nature." The question is whether this position makes possible (necessary?) a doctrine of the Trinity.

54. Among the recent proposals in American theology for a con-

temporary reformulation of the doctrine of the Trinity note especially the brief reference in Peter C. Hodgson, *Jesus—Word and Presence*, and the more extensive discussion in Robert W. Jenson, *God After God* (New York: Bobbs-Merrill, 1969). See also Jenson's *Story and Promise* (Philadelphia: Fortress Press, 1971), pp. 103–129. Whereas Hodgson suggests that the word-character of God leads us to conceive of the divine being as "presence," "personal," and "revelation," a description which is "intrinsically triune or trinitarian in structure" (*Jesus—Word and Presence*, p. 120), Jenson seeks to portray the Trinity in temporal and linguistic terms by arguing that God is "Spirit, Father and Son: Future, Past and Present . . . Self-understanding, Language and Utterance" (*God After God*, p. 191). See my review of Jenson's position in *USQR* 26, no. 2 (Winter, 1971), pp. 171–175.

55. *HP*, p. 17 (*PT*, p. 27).

56. Although Moltmann affirms a *theopoiesis*, following classical usage, the notion of eschatological promise is more congruent with the idea of ultimate fulfillment as "humanization" than as "deification." On this point see Paul Lehmann, *Ethics in a Christian Context* (New York: Harper & Row, 1963), pp. 105–108. Much depends here upon whether one sees the πάντα ἐν πᾶσιν of 1 Cor. 15:28 as "all in all" or "everything to everyone."

57. Moltmann does write as follows: "As the force that glorifies, the Holy Spirit is also the power of unification." *CS*, p. 60 (p. 77). But elsewhere: "Man and the world are not divinized but they participate in the divine life. However, both glorified man and the glorified creation are finite, though no longer mortal, and temporal, though no longer transitory." "Creation As Open System," in *Creation, Christ and Culture: Studies in Honour of T.F. Torrance*, (Edinburgh, 1976) (pp. 119–134), p. 130.

58. "Theology As Eschatology," *The Future of Hope*, p. 11.

59. *RRF*, p. 107 (*PT*, p. 146).

60. Augustine's familiar utterance in the first chapter of the *Confessions*, ". . . Our hearts are restless till they find rest in Thee," is often cited as the *locus classicus* for an acknowledgment of a natural religious sense common to all human creatures.

61. *RRF*, p. 217.

62. Ibid.

63. *PT*, p. 186.

64. *TH*, p. 276 (pp. 253–254).

65. Rom. 8:22–23.

66. This fact is not sufficiently recognized in the following statement by Rubem A. Alves in *A Theology of Human Hope* (Washington: Corpus Books, 1969): "The pure futuricity of God is a new form of Docetism in which God loses the present dimension and therefore becomes ahistorical. . . . It is because the Spirit is present that the reality of the presence of the future, the groaning of travail and the reality of hope are created. We hope, we are determined for the future, because we are pregnant. We are 'infected' with the presence of the future. . . . Moltmann's understanding of the relation between pregnancy and hope is just the opposite. It is hope that creates the pregnancy, it is the vision of the future that makes man move" (pp. 94, 96 and n. 25 on p. 179). Actually, it is "promise" that produces the "pregnancy" of which Alves speaks in the biblical view—neither "hope," nor present experience. As "promise" this has nothing to do with "pure futuricity" in any ahistorical sense. It is the idea of "Spirit" conceived apart from promise which is the Docetic position. Alves' reading of Moltmann's position does, however, illustrate the ambiguity in Moltmann's theory itself.

67. *TH*, p. 270 (p. 248).

68. *Sendung* is a major ontological concept in the Trinitarian proposals of Moltmann's most recent writings where the *missio* is not always grounded as explicitly as earlier in the *promissio*.

69. *TH*, p. 284 (p. 262).

70. "Theology As Eschatology," *The Future of Hope*, p. 29.

71. *TH*, p. 265 (p. 243).

72. *TH*, p. 195 (p. 177). In reference to this statement Robert Jenson remarks, "Moltmann himself thinks that future-openness will end—which surely must make his project of a 'theology of hope' absurd!" (*God After God*, p. 209, n. 11.) See, however, Moltmann's more recent statement referred to in n. 74.

73. *HP*, pp. 86–87 (*PT*, p. 88).

74. Note, for example, the following passage from the essay, "Creation as Open System": "We have now described creation at the beginning as an open system and understood the historical activity of

God as that of opening up in time systems that are closed. The question now arises: Is the completion of the process of creation to be understood as the final conclusion of the open and opened systems? Is the kingdom of glory the final conclusion to the universe? . . . The consummation cannot be thought of in this way in theology. . . . Instead of a timeless eternity we should talk rather about 'eternal time'; instead of the 'end of history' we should talk rather about the end of pre-history and the beginning of the 'eternal history' of God, man and nature." *Creation, Christ, and Culture: Studies in Honour of T.F. Torrance,* p. 130.

75. Arthur Danto, *Analytical Philosophy of History,* p. 181.

76. See above, p. 5.

77. Here I am in disagreement with an assertion such as the following by H.D. Lewis, *Philosophy of Religion* (London: English Universities Press, 1965): "But what Professor Austin seems to have overlooked is the peculiarity of religious utterances. Insofar as these are about God they are about a unique Reality which falls altogether outside ordinary discourse. What holds without exception of finite things does not hold of God; He is the supreme exception, just because He is God, and this is what Professor Austin's procedures obscure," (p. 152). I am, in holding to my view, more in agreement with those Latin American liberation theologies which while addressing other issues than those which fall within the scope of this essay, and coming at the theological task from a somewhat different perspective, nevertheless equally insist upon the historical efficacy of revelation in relating the present to the future. See Gustavo Gutierrez, *A Theology of Liberation,* trans. Caridad Inda and John Eagleson (Maryknoll, N.Y.: Orbis Books, 1973), pp. 216–218 and Jose Miquez Bonino, *Doing Theology in a Revolutionary Situation* (Philadelphia: Fortress Press, 1974), pp. 139–140. Bonino writes: "Do historical happenings, i.e., historical human action in its diverse dimensions—political, cultural, economic—have any value in terms of the Kingdom which God prepares and will gloriously establish in the Parousia of the Lord? If there is such a relation, how shall we understand it? And what is its significance for our action? Juan Luis Segundo has called attention to the fact that European theologians like Moltmann and Metz explicate this relationship with words like 'anticipation,' 'sketch,' 'analogy.' 'It seems quite significant for me that none of the terms used,' says Segundo, 'contains semantically any

element of causality' '' (p. 139). And Bonino concludes, as do others, "Any extrinsic relation between Kingdom and history is insufficient to support a serious concrete engagement" (p. 140). In one respect the issue raised here by the liberation theologians is as old as the classical disputes over nature and grace. What I find germane to the subject of my inquiry, however, is that the term "promissory narration" *does* contain semantically an element of causality which provides for an intrinsic relation between kingdom and history. We are called in all the struggles of this world to signify the story. But only God can make it promissory.

78. John Searle, *Speech Acts,* p. 164.

79. Ibid., p. 198. See pp. 106–113 for Searle's analysis of the concept of "ontological commitment."

80. Arthur Danto, *Analytical Philosophy of History,* p. vii. On the explicit issue of the analysis of linguistic commitments Ian Ramsey also writes that "there arises the possibility of our associating chastened metaphysical claims with self-involving assertions." Such performative utterances, Ramsey argues, "belong to personally significant situations going beyond 'observables'." "Polanyi and J.L. Austin," *Intellect and Hope,* ed. Thomas A. Langford and William H. Poteat (Durham: Duke University Press, 1968), pp. 194–195.

INDEX OF NAMES

INDEX OF SUBJECTS

177